DEDICATION

This book is dedicated to all my clients, past and future who allow me the space to walk with them through their journey. I honor your bravery to explore the dark places and face the hard truths that often show up.

I celebrate your victories over the things that scare you, your willingness to admit the things you don't want to hear, your courage to take full ownership over some of the things that were not even yours but you needed to own to heal, your vulnerability and your joy. I wish you peace and love as you continue on your path.

And to my daughter, Jayda, you are my deepest motivation and greatest love.

Keep going.

CONTENTS

OWN YOUR SHIFT

25 ESSENTIAL PRINCIPLES FOR FINDING PEACE WITHIN A DIFFICULT LIFE

Susaye Rattigan, PhD

INTRODUCTION

I've always had great expectations for my life, the least of all was happiness. The fame and success and the grand impact on others' lives was the cherry on top. But peace was something I felt I worked hard for and really deserved. So imagine my frustration when I was sitting at 35 in a stagnant relationship, rife with arguments, control and frustration, a business that I felt was keeping me stuck in a place I had long grown tired of and a superactive 4 year-old child that I wanted to spend more time with but couldn't.

From the outside, it would seem that I was good or should have been good. I wasn't wealthy but I had enough. I was comfortable. It looked good.

Yet, on the inside was a bubbling cauldron of doubt and disappointment and a crushing fear that I would never amount to the promise that my life held. Not that it has at this moment, but sitting in the dark somewhere between 35 and 36 and wondering what the hell I was doing was not the impact I was hoping to have. I was stuck. Stagnant and living on a wheel. Work, school run, back to work, home, stress and back to work. Peace was not something that I had.

The moment I decided to quit that life and create another one came in the middle of a workshop I was giving. I was running the Design Your Life Workshop (Catch a Fire) and teaching about deconstructing your current life and taking the pieces you loved to create something new while discarding the rest. One of the central ideas of Catch a Fire is that you don't really have to burn your entire life down in one go, instead, you could take a trial life. Take a break from the life you thought you didn't want and go spend some time in the one you think you want.

The Transition to a trial life is easier said than done of course, but that idea instantly sent me feelings of regret--of selling off my entire life and moving to a country that I thought held happiness for me. Maybe I could have taken 6 months off, put my stuff in storage and ran away for 6 months. Maybe it would have satisfied my soul. I don't know. What I do know is that life teaches us many things in many ways. All things that we have to find peace with in order to be at peace. And it is a journey. Filled with tough questions, second guessing, heartache, joys and laughter, tears and pain. Through it all, we have to look for the kernels of happiness that pop up but keep aiming for the river of peace that underlies it all.

Too often when life experiences confront us on this journey we forget what we have learned. I started writing this book a number of years ago and took a break when life decided to live me instead. I traveled and resettled into a life that felt more like me. I restarted and grew a successful business. I unschooled my child and took full control of the life that was meant for me.

This was my original rationale for this book: *"I'm writing this book for myself. To help me remember that life is being lived even when it doesn't look the way I want and maybe, just maybe I can eke out a little bit of happiness and find the river of peace that runs through it."*

As I've returned to writing, I have a new rationale for writing this book. Not much has changed but I have learned a lot more since then.

The major part of this work was to remind myself of the lessons I had learned and needed to implement on my quest to finding peace.

Upon my return from a year away, exploring other ways that my life could look, I settled back into my practice. This time around, I was met by a number of women who had somehow lost their peace or had no real idea what peace was for them. They were sad and lonely and lost. They were struggling with severe anxiety, unexplained health conditions, broken relationships, a loss of purpose, deep and painful regrets and despair. I saw myself in them and felt their longing. They longed for things to make sense, to release the shame of not living their fullest lives. They desperately wanted change but were not sure how to get there. I've managed to help hundreds of women move from where they were to a place where they are able to live peaceful and happier lives. Because life is a work in progress, my goal was for these women to be able to generate practices, worldviews and solid self esteem and efficacy that would sustain them as they come upon the obstacles of life that were sure to meet them down the road.

I share with you some of the lessons that I learned and that others had to accept and practice to bring them peace in the midst of what started out as a difficult life.

"You find peace not by rearranging the circumstances of your life, but by realizing who you are at the deepest level."

—Eckhart Tolle

1

Own your story.

Your life is your story and you decide how it gets told.

Everything that you have experienced up until today has been the story of YOUR life. Even though you have shared it with others, been influenced by your family, been hurt by friends and lovers, been cheated on, been abused and assaulted by those close to you–your "villains", these experiences are yours and yours alone. How you carry these stories in your mind and live them out in your life determines how you show up and how you choose to view the world.

I am not saying you're responsible for the things that happened to you. In fact, I know you're not responsible for the majority of things that happened to you. I am saying; however, that you are responsible for the story that you tell about your life. You are responsible for the meaning that you make from the things that have happened to you. You are fully responsible for what you do with the stories that have formed the book of your life.

If you're like many of us, you have defined your life and limited yourself by the experiences that you have had. While your experiences have formed the foundation of who you are, you are always adding new bricks and, ultimately, new levels to the life you're building. Your duty is to use the foundation in the best ways that you can.

One way to use your experiences to your benefit is to tell the stories of your life in brand new ways. Most people who have succeeded at creating big shifts in their lives have learned how to reframe their experiences in ways that empower and embolden them. What is common in the stories of others who have not found success is the stories they keep telling themselves in which they are the lead victim. They have failed to reframe their experiences in ways that couch their experiences in lessons that can be used in empowering ways.

One other feature you will find in disempowering stories is the constant retelling of the story over and over again without any evidence of learning or growth. From a trauma processing perspective, retelling one's story is beneficial to the extent that each retelling unearths new information that shows growth. In most of the chronically disempowering stories; however, there is never any evidence that a positive lesson has been learned.

In my client work, my quest is to help clients recreate their life stories in a way that not only empowers them but allows them to be the main character of their own story. In session, I often ask clients the following questions:

- Is this the story you want to tell of yourself and your life?
- How much longer do you want to retell this same story?
- How do you want your story to be told by your children and grandchildren?
- Do you want to be the endless victim who pined away and died without ever becoming the victor or do you want a story of triumph?

Most clients give an emphatic "No!" and begin the process of claiming their stories for themselves and their own benefit. And it helps them begin to shift into living a life that is uniquely theirs.

The point at which you decide to tell a different story doesn't mean that your story changes. It does not mean that the things that have happened to you will magically disappear. It does mean that you become intentional about how you view your experiences, how you look for and extract meaning from the things you endured and how you craft your view of yourself and your life so that it becomes firm ground for you to build on.

Habit to Peace: Tell your story the way you want to remember it.

Choose the story that you want your life to tell. Imagine that you are on your deathbed and you are looking back over your life. It has been a good one; one that you are proud to have lived. What have you experienced? How have your experiences bolstered you? What are the lessons that you have learned from what you have gone through?

Practical Steps to Peace:

1. Create a timeline of your life as you remember it. Start before birth and list the conditions of your birth. What factors were present that affected your life before you were even born?
2. Identify important points along the timeline of your life as you were told or remember.
3. Try to remember the details of each individual event as it happened. Fill in the blanks that you don't remember with details told to you. Identify the ways that these events contribute to the person you know yourself to be—the positives and the negatives. Identify your strengths and weaknesses. Try to see them as building blocks of the person you now are.
4. Repeat this process making adjustments to your life events as you would want them to be. Take creative liberty with the details. This is your story after all. Replay the events in your mind until they no longer seem foreign to you. Your mind is

powerful so don't be alarmed if you find yourself having emotions about the new parts of your story.

5.   When you are satisfied, write the story of your life on paper. Try to be as descriptive and detailed as possible. Remember you get the freedom to tell your story exactly how you want it told. Reread it as much as you'd like.

"Peace is a daily, a weekly, a monthly process, gradually changing opinions, slowly eroding old barriers, quietly building new structures."

—John F. Kennedy

2

Be Present In Your Life

Have you ever sat and thought until your head hurt? Searching, rattling your mind for the answer? If anything can be compared to self-imposed hell, I would say this process is. Imagine seeing life as a distraction from finding the answer to the questions that your mind is asking; Stealing minutes from your work, from your love making, from your quality time with your spouse, to put some more energy into finding the answer, because maybe this time something will click and you'll finally be able to find the peace that has long eluded you.

There is a saying--that peace is wherever you are. This means that if you're caught up in the cycle of endless searching for answers, peace can never be where you are.

Buddhism has always appealed to me for this reason. The anticipation that at some point I can shut down my mind and actually pay attention to my breath without trying to find the next thing to do, the next way to make money, the next solution to my daughter not eating or sleeping at nights, wondering what else I could have done to save my relationship or what I can do now to find the right partner, grow the right social media account, write this book so it's perfect. And then the research...the never ending research to find more data, get more ideas, get the right cover, to assuage my fears that I'm doing it wrong.

And it never ends.
My brain never shuts off.

As the years flew by and I got older and less full of zest for the life I'm living, I had to stop and ask myself--What is the purpose of all of this questing? How does constantly being on the hunt for a different future, and never paying attention to my present, serve me? I realized that the constant striving, without mindfulness and presence served to keep me tangled in a ball of stress, unable to appreciate the things I had, unable to be satisfied with life, and feeling like a constant failure.

And then, I had a moment when I knew I couldn't go any further. One day as I stood looking in the mirror at the flaws in my body, I realized that even though I was getting older, the things I had been dissatisfied with myself about years ago hadn't changed. I was still dissatisfied with myself and had been so for such a long time. Nothing had changed even though years had gone by. In that instant, I understood that if I never stopped this cycle, I would end up an old woman still staring at her flaws in the mirror.

I stood there and tried to see myself with new eyes. Who I saw looking back at me was the person I was never pleased with, who could never do enough right, who could never accomplish enough and lived with constant prodding to be better, be prettier, be skinnier, do more. I tried to see myself as I was inside--someone who was trying really hard with the very best intentions; someone who was doing her best. I stood there for about 30 minutes showing appreciation to each part of my body--the parts I couldn't ever bring myself to like. I stared at them and touched them, trying to pour love on them and uttered positive affirmations that even if I wasn't there now that I was willing to love them.

After I did that, I asked myself a question that shifted my perspective and allowed me to begin to drop the unrealistic expectations I had of myself.

The question was: ***If nothing about my life ever changed from what it is now, could I be happy with my life?***

I rolled over in my mind the things I had– material, emotional, spiritual, social–and I concluded that I could. I could be happy with this life. Not that I would never strive for anything else, but I could be okay right now just as I am. And the practice began. Of daily being present in my life. Of appreciating what I had and loving the moments. Of loving my child. Of letting go of things I hoped would change but had shown little promise. Of no longer getting super upset with everyone else who wasn't showing up for me as I wanted them. And I began to show up for myself. Treat myself the way I wanted to be treated. Managing my expectations of others and choosing joy!

This can apply to you and your life as well. Are you being present in this life that YOU are living? It is important to remember in the day to day happenings, that even though you may do most (if not every) thing for others, that you need to carve out a space to live the life that is yours. It starts with being an active participant in your life.. By recognizing that these moments that are flying by are moments of YOUR life and once they are gone, they will never return. Once you start to be present in the NOW, you can validate whether it is what you want it to be or there needs to be big changes happening around here.

Habit To Peace: Live in the Moment You are currently in.

The Buddhists will tell you that you only have one moment--this one. Ekhart Tolle's book, *The Power of Now*, highlights the importance of remaining grounded in the present moment, but something that's even more important is being able to be satisfied at the place where you currently are. No matter what it looks like. Many people worry that if they let themselves accept their current life that it will demotivate them and get in the way of aspiring for greater. I beg to differ and offer an alternate perspective--being dissatisfied in the present predicts dissatisfaction in the future. The future that you're counting on will never look and feel like you think it will. You have to be able to appreciate life, whatever it brings. Being able to rest and be happy with what you have allows you to cultivate appreciation for it now. It allows you to practice gratitude as a habit. Once you're able to do it now, you will be able to appreciate or at least be at peace with whatever comes.

Habit to Peace: Blessing Counting.

Gratitude and the act of seeking it in our daily lives offers us an opportunity to tune into the little bricks that keep us in joy. When we neglect gratitude, everything becomes a hindrance and a bother, and peace remains elusive. The simple act of acknowledging the things in our lives that are good, or acceptable or even just saying thank you for the things that we have makes a huge difference in our perspective. It takes the focus off the things that are wrong and places the attention squarely where it belongs (at least for a few minutes)--on the things that are going right.

At least once a day (and I would encourage more than once) or whenever you get tempted to complain, that you stop, take out a sheet of paper and list as many blessings as you can think of in the next minute. Then take the next minute or two to savor each one, whispering a word of appreciation for it. It could be something as simple as "thank you." And then get back to whatever you were doing. It will change your perspective. Live in the moment you're in now. You only have this moment. Yesterday is gone and tomorrow may never come.

Practical Steps To Peace:

1. Put down the phone and computer and look at the other person. As technology becomes tethered to our persons, we have neglected the people and relationships right in front of us. While technology keeps us connected to the larger world, relationships keep us connected to our souls. And they require feeding and watering. Choose to make the people in front of you feel respected and seen. Water them.

2. Savor things. Your meal, your drink, your shower. We are in the instant age; instant happiness, instant conversations, instant this and that. Our ability to savor things is slowly being eroded. We become impatient if the water bottle takes too long to fill up. But it is essential to remember that Not everything needs to be rushed. A great deal of our power lies in being able to control our own time, slowing down ourselves and our actions so that we can actually enjoy them. Time isn't something we can get back and so being able to take our time is more of a gift than most of us realize. Use the developmental periods as a guide. Too often we see this in children who don't understand that while childhood is short, adulthood is loooong and most are never prepared for it. The teenage (adolescent) years are meant for exploration and

development of one's identity. You *should* be lost and trying to find yourself. There's no need to rush it. The 20s will help to solidify that identity and the 30s will clarify who you have really decided to be.

Every decade is a step towards getting to know yourself and solidifying your own opinions and beliefs. As you get older, you *should* care less. So for right now, be content in the season of life that you are and live in that.

3. Try to find the good things that are present in your current environment. And focus your attention on enjoying them. We each have the power of focus and like the common self development adage says, " what you focus on grows." If you shift your perspective to finding the good or unique things you have in your life now, you may realize it has more than you've been giving it credit for. But it also allows you to be at peace with where you are. Most of us are constantly wishing to be somewhere else. We engage in future casting so much that we never live in the present. We are always on the hunt for the future. And there's nothing wrong in planning for the future, but every day in the future will be that day's present. Our inability to remain focused on where we are is debilitating--mostly because we don't yet have the ability to forecast accurately and so it will never live up to our expectations. Continuous future casting doesn't allow us to

live the life that we have now. And this breeds discontent, a prime enemy of peace.

"Never be in a hurry; do everything quietly and in a calm spirit. Do not lose your inner peace for anything whatsoever, even if your whole world seems upset."

—Saint Francis de Sales

3

Save yourself, Nobody's coming to Save You.

This is a tough lesson that everybody has to learn. I try to teach my daughter this lesson that even at 5 years old, when I try my best to rescue her, there will be times that I am just not able to and she has to be able to help herself.

Now a lot of adults have grown up shrouded under the Prince or Princess Charming fantasy. Not that there are no Prince and Princess Charmings, but it's essential to know that even if they show up to save you, you have a part to play in saving yourself. No one is going to just gather you up and do the hard work of saving you while you lounge around.

Now this is a pretty fairytale-ish way of approaching this principle, but the truth is that this applies in every arena of life, whether it is romantic relationships, school, work or achievement. The only people who are doing the work for you while you take credit are getting paid. It is never free.

I can't count the number of times I have sat wishing my work would just up and do itself. And it has never happened. What has happened is that I've waited until the last minute and had to use my supergirl skills to pull it off, ending up tired, stressed and worn out. Was it necessary? No! Was it worth it! Yes and No. But the point is that no matter how much help I got, I still had to do the work myself.

And in this, your one life, your lessons are specially curated for you. They are meant for your growth and development and no-one can grow for you. No one can think for you. You have to step up and take full ownership for your life, your lessons, your successes and your failures. This is all you, my friend. You are crafting a masterpiece and the trials and errors will only make you better if you face them and extract the lessons from them.

Some of us will falter with this principle because we fail to accept that the responsibility for what happens in our lives falls squarely on our shoulders. If you think that the things that happened to you are not your fault, you would be in good company. This was something that took me a long time to accept as well. I couldn't understand how the abuse I suffered when I was younger was my fault. I couldn't understand how the things my parents did that hurt me were my fault. But I think I missed the whole point.

My life is largely a result of my perception and my willingness to act in accordance with the understanding that no matter what was done to me at the end of the day, my path to peace lies with me. The moment that I choose otherwise, I give away my power to someone else and lose the lesson available to me. Sometimes I think of life as a video game filled with one ups, extra stars and growing mushrooms (shoutout to Super Mario). People and situations are always throwing things on our path and we can either stop and blame them for doing it or find ways to jump over them and power up our skills so that we can defeat them and grow ourselves up. It is 100% our call.

As such, what we do with the things that happened to us and the situations that present themselves to us are ours to do whatever we choose with. Too many of us, refuse to accept this and end up living a life based on blame. Living from a place of blame, takes away a very precious opportunity from us--the opportunity to turn pain into prosperity, To turn mess into messages and massive impact. I'm not saying that your parents didn't do anything wrong or that you caused things to happen to you. There's a whole school of thought based on that (hello LOA folks) and while there may be some truth to that, the gold in this principle is that all of those things are par for the course of life. No one makes it out alive and no one makes it out unscathed. But the money question is: what do you do with that? Sit down and blame everyone and everything or use it and grow. The posttraumatic growth literature in psychology essentially says that even the most traumatic experiences can birth enormous growth in individuals.

Dr. Viktor Frankl, author of Man's Search for Meaning also talks about the importance of taking responsibility for your life even amidst the torture of the Holocaust. If people can survive horrible torture and go on to use their experiences to make a difference in the life of others, you can at least begin to own and accept that you have the responsibility to do something with yours.

I can't do it for you. Even as your therapist, I can only help you do it for yourself. But you are the one that has to do the work. You have to walk in your life every day. You know when and where it hurts and only you can apply the salve every day. I can only show you what salve will help.
The path to peace isn't an easy one and I hope I didn't give you false hope. It's going to be work to get it and work to keep it--much like anything else worth keeping.

And a bit of tough love--blaming everything that happens to you on others is not a good look. In fact, it is a narcissistic trait. One that serves to shift responsibility and gaslight others. It's a very bad habit and can bring you no good. This life is yours. It is your game, Your race, your fight. You HAVE to own it. Or someone else will be happy to do it for you and you won't win at the end of the day because no one plays for the other person to win in any real game. So give yourself a fighting chance and get in the game.

Habit to Peace: Make ownership a daily practice

Write yourself a letter today, taking full ownership and acceptance over your life. Keep it close by And read it frequently until you start to believe it. Nothing beats repetition in installing a habit, especially thought-based habits.

Practical Steps to Peace: Maintaining Your Ownership

1. Pay attention to those times when you slip back into blaming others. Ask yourself why it was important to shift ownership in that particular situation. What did you have to lose or gain? The point is to maintain a conscious awareness of your motivations, to decrease the habit of blaming and increase your experiences of ownership.

2. Give your victim part a name and call it by its name when it rears its head. For example, your victim part could be Belle The Blamer. When she pops up, identify her and see her for who she is. She's blaming AGAIN. The fact that you are able to be the detached observer will help you see blaming for what it is-- a bad habit that takes away your power.

"If you are depressed you are living in the past, if you are anxious you are living in the future, if you are at peace, you are living in the present."

—Lao Tzu

4

You Are Not Alone

Nobody is exempt. Everybody has something that they're worrying about, stressed about and wanting to be different. Don't be fooled by people's outward appearances. Sometimes the best dressed and most put-together people are the ones hiding the most struggle.

Life is hard. If no one ever told you or you haven't figured it out as yet. You're welcome. It can be a slog sprinkled with beautiful moments, great relationships, joy and excitement. It can also be a doldrum, full of loss, hurt pain, heartache, disappointment, tears, fears, mental and emotional issues, and trauma.

We often get trapped when we see our lives as something special and unique that no-one else could ever understand. We look at Facebook or Instagram and see beautiful pictures of others living great lives, doing big things and we look at our measly little lives and feel like we are not enough. That our lives could never live up to it and might as well be thrown away.

We misinterpret our struggles as definitive of our worth and believe that because it doesn't feel good, it is not good.

So I want to declare myself the bringer of bad news. Nobody's life is perfect. None of the pretty and shiny things you see on Facebook and Instagram are the sum total of anyone's life. No matter how many happy, beautiful moments you see plastered on social media, there are as many or even more not so happy, not so shiny moments behind the scenes. People usually show the best parts of their lives, while they hide the worst.

Your life is not the only one that has hiccups and hurdles that you have to get through. In fact, everyone else's is like that too.

You, my darling, are not alone.

Take for example, the fact that I am writing this from a cute little beach chalet in Cherating, Malaysia. I am writing on my computer on the verandah. My 5 year old is playing with her dolls beside me. She has a porcelain mug that she is using to transport water from the sink to her doll's bath. She drops the cup and I tell her to be careful. I then ask her to bring it to me. She does (point for me), but as she does, she slips and falls and the cup breaks. (ugh). This comes on the back of breaking the fan that I had to replace two days before (none of which belong to me). In that moment, my first instinct is to check whether she is cut and bleeding but my next thought is that life sucks and can it get any worse. Never mind that 1 minute ago, my life was perfection. In that moment, I was the worst Mom in the world and had the worst luck in the world. That was less than 2 minutes apart. Had I posted a picture of my location and an apt commentary, someone may have thought that my life was perfect and I only have amazing experiences. Not so my friend. I have crappy experiences like you and everyone else. Nevertheless, that was just a little example.

When I look back at my life, there are few experiences that someone has had that I haven't. This makes me a good therapist because I can empathize and have healed through those things so I can give real live tools that can help. But It also means some pretty crappy things have happened to me--from child abuse starting around age 3, to physical and emotional abuse in my family, to toxic and abusive relationships, eating disorders, low self-esteem, attempted rape, foster care--the works. Life hasn't served me a platter of roses but it has taught me quite a bit that has proven invaluable. As a result, I can help many people experiencing many things.

My experiences make me realize that you don't have to be special or chosen to experience good or bad things, that there are many more people on this earth who have lived lives like mine, better than mine, and far worse than mine. Struggle is a part of the human experience.

My experiences don't make me less or more than anyone else. It reminds me that I am human and there are no guarantees that I will have a carefree life. To the extent that I can control things, I can create that for myself.

While no one has experienced the constellation of things that you have—your particular mix of experiences are yours alone—due to the fact that we all think and see things differently, someone somewhere has experienced what you are experiencing before or will sometime later. You are not alone in the world even though it may seem like it. I can't count the number of times that I felt like I was by myself, that no-one could relate. It wasn't until I sat through hundreds of therapy sessions and heard similar things from the mouths of clients from all walks of life that I realized the human experience, while varied, is not unique to any one human. No human has life set up for them in such a way that all they experience is all good or all bad. We all have obstacles and if we are able to understand that, when the obstacles arise, we will be better able to manage them. If we are able to appreciate that after the bad times, there will be some peace again, we are likely to thrive through our tough times.

Habit to Peace: Live without Attachment

The Buddhist approach to experiencing life without attachment is a helpful one. Because we lack the ability to see what the future holds, we cannot attach a weight of good or bad to anything that happens to us. What may look good now, may have a negative effect later and what may seem negative now, may be exactly what creates a great opportunity in the future. Practice experiencing your life without attaching a good or bad descriptor.

Practical Tips to Peace:

1. Read the 4 Agreements. This is an amazing text that details 4 steps to living a good life. It helps you to reframe your approach to life and promises peace.

2. Journal about your experience. It is guaranteed that whatever you are experiencing now will change. Have a space where you can process your thoughts and feelings now and are able to return and see your growth after it shifts.

3. Be willing to offer yourself an alternate way to view your experience. Sometimes, the stories we tell ourselves about our experiences keep us stuck. Ask yourself if there is an alternate way that you can view your experience--a way that would not make it suck so bad. I wouldn't recommend lying to yourself but we are creative beings who can give all kinds of things new meaning–why not now?

4. Share your experiences with someone else. Too often we keep our struggles to ourselves. Someone else may be going through the same things and may have tips. Also, support groups and therapy are excellent resources if life feels overwhelming for you or you feel truly alone.

"Peace is the result of retraining your mind

to process life as it is, rather than as you

think it should be."

—Wayne W. Dyer

5

Forgive Your Parents

Forgiveness is harder than it sounds but it is for your benefit. The trauma research shows that our bodies hold onto the hurts and pains that we experience emotionally In his book, the body keeps the score, Dr. Bessel von Der Kolk reminds us that when trauma (or we'll just use difficult and painful emotions as a euphemism) does not get processed, it resides in our bodies. And when we carry negative emotions in our bodies, they wear on our emotional and physical sense of well-being. When we are under stress and in sadness, our immune systems become depressed and we are not able to fight off viruses and infections as effectively. Now imagine harboring deep tensions, hurts and pains for years. The effect of holding onto them sits like a ton of bricks in your body. You may not feel it every day but your body does. Forgiveness allows us to decrease and eventually release that 5 ton brick until we are no longer carrying that weight around--because as they say, holding onto pain is like drinking poison and expecting that someone else will die. Practice forgiveness for its healing powers to you. It's full time to be selfish. Do it for your own well-being even if no-one knows you're doing it. It's not about them.

Our parents can be some of the people who hurt us the deepest and as a result, we have a complex relationship with forgiving them. Even when we have forgiven strangers for deep hurts, we still struggle with forgiving our parents. Being that our parents are our first "gods" we often see them as infallible and expect that they have it all together enough that they would never do significant damage to us. And when they do, we become heartbroken. When my daughter was 3 years old, she saw me in a moment of uncontrolled anger. The look on her face was heartbreaking and the pained way that she bawled into my hug was deep and mournful. She later disclosed that I had broken her heart, and I believe her. In that moment I went from someone who would never hurt her to someone who could hurt her significantly. I lost a little bit of my shine that day, I know.

The secret to forgiving your parents is to see them as people, just like you. They were struggling to learn the same lessons you are struggling to learn now. Some manage better than others, but they did the best they could.

My journey to making peace with my childhood and my relationship with my parents wasn't an easy one. For years it was filled with feelings of being done wrong and hurt, pain and accusations. But that was when I was young and hadn't really lived or had the joy (?) of parenting a child. Really, my beliefs about blaming others had to shift because I quickly realized that everyone is in this one life trying to do the best that they can. Children do not come with a manual. There is no innate guidance about what to do with the child you have in front of you. More importantly though, your parents more than likely, learned to parent from their parents. And what happens, despite our best intentions to do differently than they did, is that we often revert to the ways of parenting that are written into our bones from the years of parenting we received.

Yes, we have a responsibility to do better than our parents did and despite what our parents did, is it possible that they did better than their parents did? Can you revise your perspective to include understanding the dynamics of your parents' experiences while they were parenting you? What level of life skills did they possess? What environment were they living in at the time? What were their stress levels? Were they working, could they provide for you? What social support networks were available to them? How was their emotional and mental health? Did they experience trauma? Although their experience of struggle or difficulties do not excuse their behaviors, in our quest for peace, understanding another's perspective and giving grace for their experiences is a skill that pays back dividends. No time is this more beneficial to you than when you are applying it to your parents. No, this does not mean that you have excused their behavior or their choices, it just means that you can place the responsibility for carrying whatever burdens are associated with your childhood where they belong--in the past-- and get to the business of healing yourself (if you need to and I have a belief that we all need to).

I also understand that some offenses by parents are difficult, almost impossible, to understand. Some have created huge caverns in our souls, deep scars in our hearts and unspeakable pain. Yet, we have a responsibility to ourselves to free ourselves from the things that can keep us trapped in years of pain. Healing really is our responsibility and while our parents may have been wrong and may still not be able to acknowledge our view of their roles, they do not have to. You have to be willing to accept that. You can't make anyone do anything and if they are not in a place in their growth to take responsibility for their behaviors, that is fine. Your life is your responsibility. Your childhood was your reality and people are allowed to see things differently. What happened affects you. No-one else but you has to live with it. Everybody has their price to pay. There's very little need to make someone else pay the price you believe they should. No one else can free you but you.

Habit to Peace: Let your parents Be human

Try to see your parents as another person, equal to you, with the same existential struggle--trying to be human in the best way that they know how. They may be older but who knows, you may know more than them. Shift your perspective from them being the people who knew better to seeing them as people who were trying to survive life in the ways they knew.

Practical Steps to Peace: Begin the process of forgiveness.

1. Acknowledge that your parents are human, just like you and were doing the best that they could have. Given the circumstances of their lives and what they believed, they couldn't have done any better than they did--even if you believe they could.

2. Try to understand them as people and then accept that they do not have to own anything that you believe that they should about how life was for you. This was your experience and it affects you. Decide what aspects of the experience you are willing to carry around and release the rest.

3. Take a few minutes to bring their faces to memory or their essence (if you're not ready for faces as yet) and then send them good wishes from your place of understanding.

4. Know that you do not have to engage or welcome them with open arms. This process is for you, not them. What you do is a direct result of the level of comfort that YOU have around engaging.

5. Don't expect that your forgiveness means anything will change in terms of their behavior or ownership of your experience. Your mission is peace, not magic.

"Offer your forgiveness with the intention that it will free you from unnecessary pain. Don't expect that your forgiveness means anything will change in terms of another's behavior or another's ownership of your experience. Your mission in forgiving is getting yourself to peace, not creating magic."

—Dr. Susaye

6

Be Teachable.

One of the best traits any person can have is the willingness to learn and grow and ultimately change. When I refer to being teachable, I mean the willingness to take what someone else says and evaluate it and use it. In relationships, we want our partners to be teachable-- we want them to heed our counsel, listen to our advice and consider its usefulness. In our work, our bosses and colleagues want us to be able to receive feedback and use it constructively. When we are obtuse and unwilling to learn, we create a stagnant environment where change is hard and cooperation is like pulling teeth.

One important thing to remember is that most people are lost. The majority of us humans are not asking ourselves good questions. We are not actively trying to grow. As a result, we end up reliving the same patterns over and over, wondering why life doesn't change or

get any better for us. We miss the cues that there are lessons to be learned in our day to day lives because we are not looking for them; we are not actively seeking to learn. Oftentimes, our lessons are forced
upon us because we refuse to go in search of them. And ultimately, we are blindsided by the harsh realities because we have not been paying attention.

One of the biggest challenges in modern relationships is the conviction that most of us have that we already know what we need to know--because life, religion, parents or education has taught us. We accept the assumptions of living as commandments and never question. Over time, we explain away our habits as "just who I am." What has happened to you, if you have heard yourself utter these words, is that you have closed down and are no longer open to growing and changing.

The fact is that most people seem to believe that their way is right and will argue continuously for their point without consulting any evidence. One of the famous Greek Philosophers stated that " An unexamined life is a life not worth living." While this is pretty strong language, it highlights the stagnation that not subjecting yourself and life to scrutiny often brings.

One of the first ways I realized that I was different was that I was willing to examine the beliefs that were passed down to me. Sometimes it was challenging because it made me the odd one out in a number of situations but it allowed me the time to explore other schools of thought and evaluate them based on my own life experience. In addition, it allowed me to experiment and test their veracity. By doing this, I realized that there are many truths. And many ways to get to truth. And that *my* truth isn't always *the* truth. This further allowed me to step back and give others the opportunity to live their truths without feeling the need to attack or judge. Life has many ways of teaching us and none of us have the same path. It is more important that we are constantly trying to learn–that we are teachable.

Ignoring this fact will set you up for a world of hurt, especially in your relationships with others. When you are able to decipher the behaviors of those who are open and teachable, you can choose better for yourself and your life. It is your responsibility, if you want peace in your life, to know the behaviors of people who are not open to learning, questioning, growing and changing. It will save you a great deal of frustration. A person who refuses to grow, will not respond favorably to your identification of their need to change. A person who has accepted themselves as fixed, does not believe that they can change and more than likely does not want to change. Just the mere belief that they cannot change diminishes the likelihood that they would even try. So save yourself the heartache. Your challenge is to remain open and teachable. Since you are reading this book, I believe that you are open to change and that's a beautiful thing.

Habit to Peace: Remain teachable

If you want to be more teachable, stay humble. See everyone who offers you advice as an equal or a valuable asset. Give ear to what others are saying, even if you disagree with someone, taking the time to listen and trying to understand a new perspective will help you learn. That is what being teachable is all about.

Practical Steps to Peace: Remaining Teachable

Evaluate your teachability: **Ask yourself, "Am I really teachable?"**
All the good advice or therapy or coaching in the world won't help you if you are not teachable. To know whether you are *really* open to new ideas and new ways of doing things, ask yourself the following questions:

1. Am I open to other people's ideas?
2. Do I listen more than I talk?
3. Am I open to changing my opinion based on new information?
4. Do I readily admit when I am wrong?
5. Do I observe before acting on a situation?
6. Do I ask questions?
7. Am I willing to ask a question that will expose my ignorance?
8. Am I open to doing things in a way I haven't done before?
9. Am I willing to ask for directions?

10. Do I act defensive when criticized, or do I listen openly for truth?

If you answered no to one or more of these questions, then you may not be as teachable as you can be to allow yourself to reach your growth and development goals. This means that there's an opportunity for you to develop in how teachable you are. You need to soften your attitude, learn humility, and remember the words of John Wooden: "Everything we know we learned from someone else!"

"Most people want to hear or tell a good story. But they don't realize they can and should be the good story. That requires intentional living."

— John C. Maxwell

7

Be Intentional.

I missed this lesson for a long time. It seemed to come close and then take a step back. The first real contact I had with this was when a friend of mine asked me what my intention was for a new relationship I was entering. I was blank. I had no idea what my intention was and the truth was I had no intention. I remember her saying that intention was the compass for where the relationship would go and we needed to get clear on what that was before we went any further, if we went any further. I didn't quite get the lesson then. Over the years though, I have come to realize the importance of being intentional in everything that I do. Without intention, I end up lost and wavering; looking for direction. Intention also serves to guide the decisions I take and whether they are in alignment with who I am and the goals I have at any point. If I start with intention,

I am more likely to finish. And if I don't finish, it's because I have realized that I no longer hold that intention.

In general, you can think about intention as being mindful or present with yourself as you make choices or have experiences, with the end goal of being able to remain true to your values and what matters to you. When I think of intention, I think of someone who is living intentionally is someone who has chosen to remain authentic to themselves and their own goals, aspirations and experiences. Instead of living by anyone else's rules and society's suggestions, an intentional person has chosen to identify their own values and choose based on their values. Living intentionally is letting go of all the things you have been taught to go after to validate your worth and instead choosing the things that make you feel good based on your core beliefs.

Intention tends to trump chance in my book. Things happen by chance (50% of the time), intention allows you to create goals, set a plan and work towards it. Intention creates opportunity and results more than 50% of the time.

You need to have an intention for everything you do. Doing something without intention gets you lost quickly and very close to lost is the feeling of despair. Before you do something stop and think: what is the purpose behind me doing this? What would I like to accomplish?

Habit to Peace: Be Intentional about Your Actions

Be intentional about your actions. Before you do anything, identify the intention behind it. Sometimes an intention can be as simple as I just want to have fun, but know that there are consequences attached. So when the consequences come, take ownership of them as you did the intention. If you choose to act without intention, then expect whatever comes your way. No-one ever got to a specific destination without intention, you don't just drift there. You have to be deliberate about where you're going even if you're letting the universe or God guide you.

Practical Tips to Peace: Maintain Intentionality

1. Write the intentions for your life, daily. This is like your to-do list. Read it over and allow it to serve as your guide and compass to the future you want to experience.

2. Practice active listening. It allows you to catch the intentions of others even when they are not clearly stated. Few people will openly and honestly share their intentions. Someone with clear intentions will say and act in accordance. Someone with poor intentions, will often act contrary to what they say, so pay attention to actions.

3. Engage in self reflection and self examination. Spend 5 or 10 minutes every day reviewing the actions and words that you have used and their alignment with what you aim to accomplish and to represent. Are you in alignment, what

needs to change to bring you closer to who you want to be and how you want to live?

4. Identify Your Core Values. Your values guide what intentional decision-making looks like for you. Sit with yourself and revisit the three most important experiences that you have had in your life. What are the feelings that you had in those experiences that made them most important. These are likely linked to your core values.

   a. Who do you admire? This could include people you know personally, famous figures, characters in a book, etc.

      i. As you think about these people, write down:

      ii. what it is about them that inspires you

      iii. the admirable qualities they possess

      iv. behaviors and actions you would like to emulate

   b. What inspires you to take action?

      i. Often our core values reveal themselves through our actions. Can you think of a situation when you took a stand for someone or something?

      ii. Try writing down some of the reasons you felt so strongly to take action. For example:

         1. the feelings that motivated you to speak up or act

         2. what you were willing to risk in that situation

3. the results of taking action — what you gained or lost

    c. When do you feel most like yourself? When you're in situations that allow you to be authentic, that's a clue that you are in alignment with your values. And when you have to betray yourself to fit in or find success, you feel ashamed and alone.

In situations that feel wrong in some way, what's going on? Write down:

    i. who you're with

    ii. what feelings are triggered

    iii. what these experiences cost you emotionally or physically

Sample Core Values:

If you found it hard to put words to the qualities, emotions, and ideas in the exercises above, it may help to look through some examples.

Take some time to explore this list of values and beliefs, and consider which ones resonate with you:

Family	Freedom	Security	Loyalty	Intelligence
Connection	Creativity	Humanity	Success	Relationship
Knowledge	Patience	Change	Prosperity	Wellness
Finances	Gratitude	Grace	Joy/Play	Harmony

"We must learn to regard people less in the light of what they do or omit to do, and more in the light of what they suffer."

– Dietrich Bonhoeffer

8

Give grace and margins.

Have you ever done something to someone that you didn't mean to cause harm and they were able to understand and let it go. That was you receiving grace from the other person. When we show grace to someone, we show kindness even when the other person doesn't deserve it by our definition. Grace is going out of our way to offer compassion and love to someone who may not appreciate it or be able to return the favor.

Giving margins is pretty similar. It is the habit of allowing room for people to make mistakes. It's almost expecting that others will make mistakes and not taking it too personally. We are all humans after all. The giving of grace and margins calls us to remove the perfectionistic expectations we hold of others. We almost never expect others to make mistakes and when they do, we torture them for it. I am not espousing that you become a doormat and let people make mistakes all over you. I am encouraging you to give them space to make mistakes and show some compassion to them when they make stupid mistakes--separating the person from the action.

The ability to separate someone's being from their action is a useful trait. While it can be challenging to practice daily, it is essential that we are able to understand that our actions don't make us who we are. And likewise that another person's actions, especially infrequent, do not make them either. Our daily lives are made up of a series of grace and margins given by others.

When I found this concept I marveled at how true this was. Most of us still exist because of grace from others. We still have jobs/clients because people have seen past our mistakes and not fired (or killed) us every time we have made one.

Most people are going through something and need grace. Most people are trying their best, give them a break once in a while. And while their best may not look like the definition of best in our dictionary, it likely is the best that they are capable of at this moment. This is not a call to accept poor behavior from others. Instead it is a challenge to release ourselves from the need to judge and execute others in our minds when they have made a mistake. In the past, I have been guilty of deciding on the character of an individual from one mistake or wrong they have done to me, usually from the perspective that they were out to intentionally harm me.

WHile some people are out to intentionally harm others, sometimes, the harm we experience is largely done unconsciously or in an attempt to protect themselves. I guarantee there are people who you have unintentionally harmed. Often because one decision in one direction means someone else gets a no in another direction and we are not able to predict how another person will process that. One person may understand the decision, the other may see it as a personal slight. And on and on we go.

Even though giving grace and margins is good for your emotional well-being because you're not walking around with chips on your shoulders all day, it also bodes well for the future of many of our relationships. SO many of us are carrying around hurts from long ago, long forgotten by the perpetrators. Our burden is so heavy that every time we hear their names, our blood boils, while they go skipping on in their lives. If we were to step back and analyze the situation, we'll realize that they are quite fine, going about their business. THat in fact, we are the ones harmed by our own decisions. If we were to sprinkle just a little grace on the situation, we will be able to move forward and enjoy some peace and happiness ourselves.

Habit to Peace: Give others grace and allow a margin for errors.

Allow others the space to make mistakes and refrain from taking the behaviors of others so personally. When I was younger I had a best friend, who everybody loved. She had great relationships with almost everyone she met. Whenever I was not able to get in contact with her and finally had a conversation with her, I would often argue about her not calling me. Our conversations became tense because in my mind, she made time for everyone else, but me. As I've gotten older and busier, I completely understood why things happened the way they did. And while we're still friends, the time between our interactions have grown and I am perfectly fine with it because our friendship doesn't change because of time apart or distance. The fact that we still have a relationship is testament to the fact that my friend is excellent at giving grace and margins. She gave me the space to be young and insane (because who does that?!?) and forgave me for getting upset without me even recognizing what I was doing. That saved our friendship.

Practical Steps to Peace: Being a Grace Giver

1. Keep Short Accounts of wrongs. When you need to apologize, do it quickly. Don't keep a running total of how many times someone may have done wrong towards you. Forgive them, even if they don't ask for it. Grace can go a long way to repairing a relationship if you will respond in a loving way, even when they don't.

2. Respond With Grace: Sometimes the way that someone gives you feedback or responds to you can cause your blood to boil and a reaction from you can make the situation even worse. Usually, I say this to clients. Take a deep breath and then

allow yourself to calm down before you respond. The rationale behind this suggestion is that our immediate response is often reactionary. The deep breath, sends oxygen to our brains and allows us to respond from a place of calm. It allows us to be able to hear what is said without our personal emotional filters and respond in an appropriate way. Even when what is said is mean-spirited and harsh. You don't have to let others walk over you, but you can respond in a gracious way. Accept what they have to say and thank them for their input. Whatever they have said to you may be upsetting or hurtful but the way you respond can help the healing begin immediately. A quick response with anger will leave you seething. But the sooner you can respond with a smile and a calm spirit the sooner YOU will be able to see the truth; whatever truth is in their words and make the changes that need to be made.

"Negative people talk and your dreams begin to wither off. But they begin to sprout in the fragrance of hope when they find a new soil! Change your environment!"

Unknown

9

Manage your environment.

Your environment, which includes your friends, colleagues, location, habits and lifestyle, impacts you far more—for better or for worse—than you realize. You can't make a significant, lasting change without altering some elements of your environment.

When you are going through a difficult time, you may tend to withdraw into a space of positivity and isolation where you listen to motivational tapes and watch inspiring youtube videos. The driving force is to shut out the noise and cleanse your mental and emotional palate. This is good for emotional healing and provides short-term relief. What matters more is the environment that surrounds you daily. The parts that we don't have control of can challenge our coping skills but for those parts that are a result of our direct choices, we must intentionally craft so they serve as vehicles to better quality of life and increased peace of mind.

When you have a clear idea about who you want to be and where you want to go, It is imperative that you intentionally choose others who embody the traits and characteristics to which you are aspiring. These individuals don't have to just be friends and family members. They could include mentors, coaches, therapists, colleagues and other peers who are progressive and leaning in the direction that calls to you.

Be discerning about the people you choose to be around. The famous quote is that we are the sum total of the five people we choose to hang around. While I agree with this statement, I want to extend it a little further by including that you are also the sum of what you watch, the music you listen to and the physical, spiritual and psychological spaces that you immerse your heart, soul and mind into.

You decide what you listen to and talk about. You decide what you watch and how much of it. Whatever you allow into your environment permeates every facet of who you are. Think of it as resting your brain into a big pot of marinade (made up of the things you listen to and imbibe) for hours and hours. You may take your brain out of the marinade, but some of it has definitely soaked in.

Your life is a reflection of the things you invite into it. You have a duty to yourself to create the best space possible for yourself to thrive. It may be challenging for some who've never experienced an environment curated for their growth and well being, but on this part of the journey marked by intention and deliberate choice, you get the privilege of curating your own environments.

Don't be afraid to uninvite those things or people who do not serve you or make you feel good about yourself. You have a duty to yourself to choose wisely and to craft the physical, social, spiritual, and mental environment that supports, inspires and motivates you for the person you are striving to become and life you are committed to leading in the future.

Habit to Peace: Maintain Awareness of Your Triggers So You Can Manage Your Emotions Better

In our daily lives, we are surrounded by triggers in our environment that positively or negatively influence our behaviors. Make a habit of paying attention to the things that trigger your behavior. Once you are able to bring awareness to those triggers then you are able to intervene before they take over or stop them once they get you going. Taking a few seconds to allow yourself to breathe can be priceless in saving you from a blow up or breakdown. In addition, understanding how the people and things that you have selected for your life enhance your sensitivity to triggers will also go a far way in you being in control of your emotions. Sometimes we stay stuck and out of control because our boundaries are built around people and situations that play on our emotions and keep us off kilter.

Practical Steps To Peace: Manage Your Triggers

1. Assess who is in your top 5. Who are the 5 people that you spend the most time with? What are their goals and aspirations? What behaviors do they display? Are these in alignment with the direction in which you want your life to go?

2. Assess where you spend your time and what you actually do while in that physical space. Where do you actually spend time? What do you and others do there? How much time do you spend there and what do you accomplish? What is the vibe like? Is that the vibe you intended to experience?

3. Audit your habits and your lifestyle. What are the habits that you are displaying daily? Are these the habits you actually want to build? What does your lifestyle look like? Remember that your current habits and lifestyle predict your life in the future. If you continued in these habits, would they get you to where you want to be in the future?

4. Identify one small change that you can make that would go a long way in changing your environment. Create a plan to make the necessary changes, implement the tiny change and measure the outcome.

"When we fail to set boundaries and hold people accountable, we feel used and mistreated. This is why we sometimes attack who they are, which is far more hurtful than addressing a behavior or a choice."

— Brené Brown

10

Be okay with setting and embracing boundaries.

I come across a good number of people-pleasers. These kind and caring individuals would give their last breath to make another happy--often to the exclusion of their sense of self. Often to their own detriment. WHile you may think of this as a noble trait. It's one of the most painful traits that these individuals possess. Because often they would prefer to not be people pleasers. They understand that their drive to please others often comes from a place of insecurity, emotional manipulation (attempting to earn love and acceptance by meeting others' needs often for nothing in return, yet desperately desiring that which they don't receive). They soon come to realize that they have very little control over themselves and their lives. They frequently put themselves out of their own way to help another. They disregard their own needs to make someone else feel better. They run on empty to fill others up and they struggle to ask for help.

For many of us, this is our existence and we carry around a heavy burden--knowing we need to stop but fearing how others will feel when we are no longer the one that they can run to for everything. When I encounter an all-out pleaser, I know that our mission is to identify and successfully implement boundaries.

Boundaries are a way to take care of ourselves. They are gentle rules that indicate to ourselves and others where you stand and what you will and will not tolerate. When you understand how to set and maintain healthy boundaries, you can avoid the feelings of resentment, disappointment, and anger that build up when your limits have been pushed.

Boundaries can take many forms. They can range from being rigid and strict to appearing almost nonexistent. If you have more rigid boundaries, you might:
- keep others at a distance
- seem detached, even with intimate partners
- have few close relationships
- avoid close relationships

If you have more loose or open boundaries, you might:
- get too involved with others' problems
- find it difficult to say "no" to others' requests

- overshare personal information with others
- seek to please others for fear of rejection

Most of my pleasers have the latter--boundaries that are so porous, that they seem almost nonexistent. They are often afraid to enforce any type of boundary because enforcement undermines their identity as someone who is always available. To begin to enforce boundaries, you have to release the identity of a pleaser and become clear that you too are deserving of your own time and resources. While I know it's easier said than done, you have to begin somewhere. There are five different types of boundaries:

1. Physical. This refers to your personal space, your privacy, and your body. You might be someone who is comfortable with public displays of affection (hugs, kisses, and hand-holding), or you might be someone who prefers not to be touched in public.

2. Sexual. These are your expectations concerning intimacy. Sexual comments and touches might be uncomfortable for you.

3. Intellectual. These boundaries concern your thoughts and beliefs. Intellectual boundaries are not respected when someone dismisses another person's ideas and opinions.

4. Emotional. This refers to a person's feelings. You might not feel comfortable sharing your feelings about everything with a friend or partner. Instead, you prefer to share gradually over time.

5. Financial. This one, as you guessed, is all about money. If you like to save money — not spend it on trendy fashions — you might not want to loan money to a friend who does.

The easiest place to begin in the boundary-setting journey is to know what you want and don't want to experience and be ready to say No when you need to. Defining what you want and don't want are likely going to be the easiest parts. The challenge will show up when you have to say no and run the risk of hurting people's feelings or being made to feel like the bad guy (who is letting someone down).

For boundaries to have a strong foundation, you need to show yourself a bit of love. Boundaries will be difficult to maintain if you have a running narrative in your head that you do not deserve to have love and you are less than others, anyway. If you deem yourself as undeserving, then you're going to find it difficult to put boundaries in place that protect you. Your boundaries rest on your sense of self-love and self value. Weak self value, makes it hard to say No.

So, know this. You really don't even have to say "NO", here are some alternatives you can say:

- That doesn't work for me
- I don't think that's a good idea
- Let me think about it and get back to you
- That doesn't seem possible
- I'd rather not.

- I have another engagement.
- I'll take a raincheck.
- That is not a good fit for me.
- I know someone one else who would like this, let me see if they would be interested
  instead.

Habit to Peace: Communicate Your Boundaries and Accompanying Consequences

Communication is critical in the world of boundaries, especially if someone consistently oversteps yours. While you might need to raise your concerns, these discussions need not be confrontational. Clarity around what you actually want to experience helps you begin the process of clearly communicating what your boundaries are and as well as the consequences of overstepping them. Think of your boundaries as clear instructions about how you need to be treated to remain safe. Someone who cares about you wants you to feel safe and secure. And if they do not honor this desire, then this is information for you about how they see you and honor you.

Practical Steps To Peace: Identify and Implement Your Boundaries:

1. Write down the list of boundaries that you need for you to have a sense of being respected and cared for by those you interact with frequently.

2. Decide on what the consequences are for breaching your boundaries.

3. Communicate your boundaries to individuals as soon as possible. This may look like informing them when they cross the boundary. Detail how it makes you feel and what the consequences will be in the future. You can also identify clear boundaries and consequences and inform individuals ahead of time.

4. Enforce your consequences immediately but with love and compassion. Remember that some of these individuals do not have boundaries themselves so it will be challenging for them to honor yours. This is not to be excused, so don't backtrack. Be firm because they too need structure.

"Set the standard! Stop expecting others to show you love, acceptance, commitment, & respect when you don't even show that to yourself."

— Steve Maraboli

11

Choose yourself.

No-one else is thinking about your life as much as you are, not even your Mom. Do not be a martyr for things and people that would not martyr themselves for you.

One of the most important shifts anyone who has had a difficult, painful life can make is from choosing others to choosing themselves. If you're like so many others who have lived their lives with low self esteem, in anxiety, fear and doubt, choosing yourself is likely the last thing on your list. Life has probably taught you that in order to be lived, accepted or valued, you must choose others and put all of their needs, emotions and desires first. You've likely become a master at reading others, scavenging for any sign that they might judge or reject you. And so you've learned how to be.

To make a change from an external focus (everyone else's needs and desires) to an internal focus (your needs and desires as primary) is a difficult and frightening one. It assumes that you even know what it means to choose you. For someone who's never done it, it is like rocket science. How does one choose themself? Isn't it selfish to focus on your needs first? What about my family? Won't they suffer if I just focus on me?

Well, while those are all relevant questions, the fundamental driving force for all humans is survival and whereas you have previously thought that the most likely way for your survival was through meeting others needs, what I am going to say may shock you. You are more likely to survive if you meet your needs first.

We all know the saying "put your oxygen mask on first, before you put anyone else's on." This not only applies to airplanes. It applies to all facets of life and especially the relational. When we tend to the needs of others while neglecting our own, we do so at our own detriment. What often results is emotional starvation, spiritual burnout and loss of a sense of self. I've seen it too many times. Someone who is deeply caring and loving and wants to help everyone, yet they have no idea about what their own desires are, or what they prefer to eat, wear or do. Is this you? Do you have clarity about the things that make you tick? You can tell by your answers to the following questions:

- What are your desires and preferences?
- Do you have a self care routine?

- How do you nourish and replenish yourself? How many hours of sleep do you need? When do you work best?
- What would you do if marooned on a desert island?
- What is your dream destination?
- Do you even have any dreams anymore?

Choosing yourself makes you an all round better person. It allows you to meet your own needs, keep you reserves full so you can tend to the needs of those who you desire to help. Choosing yourself doesn't mean forsaking all others, it means prioritizing you, first. It means placing your needs, intentions, and values at the forefront of your mind and using them to guide your actions. It improves your sense of wholeness, your self esteem and your joy. It removes the burden from others to tend to your dry garden and places it squarely on your shoulders, giving you much needed autonomy and allows you to create boundaries that not only support you but offers structure for those others with whom you interact. And while society may tell you otherwise, people need structure. Everyone thrives with boundaries.

Remember that even though friends and family are an integral part of our lives, they do not form the whole of our lives. And if they do, that might be a little bit of a problem. You are an individual being with your own destiny and your own life path. You are a whole person separate from any other. You too deserve a life made up of your authentic self and your own determinations. You, like everyone else, deserve your own passions, dreams, goals and to live in a way that is authentic to you.

Habit to Peace: Pay Attention to Your Thoughts and Feelings

Pay attention to your thoughts and feelings. These are the lifeblood of your mind and your heart. They send you signals about what you truly desire as well as those things that do not bring you joy and peace. While they shouldn't become your gods or your only guides, they offer valuable insight into who you really are. Please don't mistake this for living at the mercy of your feelings; instead understand them, give ear to them and use them to inform you not to decide for you.

Practical steps to Peace: Choosing Yourself

1. Release the need to be a Super Savior for others and refocus some of the energy on yourself and your life. Examine the ways that you are showing up for others. Make a list of all the people who depend on you and then make another list of all the People who you are really able to depend on. You can follow it up with the ways that you have helped others in the past year and make a list of the ways that others have helped you. Compare the lists and evaluate whether You would like to continue showing up in the way that you have been. If you do, identify ways that you will offer support to yourself or seek support. If you don't, identity roles that you will begin to release In others' lives and how you will use that energy in your life.

2. Create a self care plan and make space in your life to implement it. Make a list of things that you would like to do to nourish your body, mind and soul. You don't have to know exactly what you will do, begin to explore ideas. Over time you will come to a space where you know what feels good to you. If you're just starting out, it's ok to just try new experiences and practices and feel out the ones that work well for you.

3. Craft a solid support system. This may be difficult if you've always been Reba the Rescuer, but you may be able to identify good finds or family who are willing to support you, if you are able to voice your needs. Write a list of the ways that you would like to be supported. Revisit the list of those who have helped or showed up for you in some fashion and identify the ones who would most likely be open to supporting you. Have a conversation letting them know what you would like from them and ask for their help.

4. Tweak this process as you go. It may work well at first but your family and friends have been used to your sacrificial ways for a while and so it may be difficult for them to adjust immediately. Some may be downright unwilling and push back. That is ok. This is where you enforce your boundaries with consequences.

"Avoiding danger is no safer in the long run than outright exposure. The fearful are caught as often as the bold."

—Helen Keller

12

Life is not something to fear.

Even the most carefully planned life goes off-course at some point. No one's life is exactly as they planned and if it is, it is way more boring than they imagined. Similarly, things aren't often as bad as we think they will be.

My early life until graduating graduate school was filled with fear. I was afraid to do anything if I wasn't certain about the outcome. I lived from a place of worry and doubt. I worried that things would go wrong and I doubted my ability to do anything about it if it did. I tried to be perfect because Christianity had taught me that God would be mad at me if I didn't have it all perfect. Plus I had told myself that there was only one way to do things. And If I didn't do it that way, my life would be a failure and failure was something that I worried endlessly about. This kind of thinking was a trap. It kept me from fully owning my life and fully living it. I stayed safe, played small and did the things other people thought were best. As a result, I felt like I wasted my 20s. While other people were living and having children, getting married and doing school I saw life as doing school and anything else was extra until real life began. I laugh now thinking about it but that was real to me.

Growing up, I felt I had little power and control over my life and life had already been so hard on me that I thought now I would try my best to control it so I could avoid adding any more hurt and pain. I remember before I moved to Jamaica, I went to see my pastor because I wasn't sure what God's will was for my life and if I would be punished for stepping out of it. I was lost and living in fear.

What living in that state of mind did to me and does to you is that it keeps you stuck. It keeps you running and hiding from the beauty that life has to offer even with all the possible struggles. What I learned over all those years was that no matter how much I tried to plan and run away and tiptoe around life, it always showed me that I wasn't doing anything special. Even when I did all I could to make a relationship work, when it was time to end, it ended. Despite my protesting. And there I was thinking, "But I did everything I could." No matter how good of a friend I was to someone else, our friendship would end and I was standing there saying "but i was such a good friend to them."

So I learned that walking the cautious life doesn't mean anything. It doesn't promise that you'll experience only good. It doesn't mean that you will never be hurt again. Instead, you live life expecting that it won't all be good and some things will turn out great and others won't. That some risks have a big reward, some have a small reward and some are crapshoots but it is in taking the risk--the experience of getting to the end that enriches your life. Had I not stepped out of fear, I probably would be living in a dark room afraid of my shadow. Never experiencing anything that the world has to offer. That is a sad way to live and cuts your life short. I can guarantee that living in fear doesn't allow you to live to your potential. In fact, it saps your life energy and attracts negative experiences your way.

What you have to remember is that life is meant to be lived, not bottled up. It still passes if we bottle it up. And instead of just being fearful, we become old and fearful. Hopeless and fearful. Sad and fearful.

Habit to Peace: Make Mindfulness a Practice

Make meditation a daily part of your living practice. Engaging in meditation allows you to be mindful and aware of what is happening in the present moment. Meditation, especially mindfulness meditation requires that you step away from the concerns about the future and ruminating over the past and sit with yourself in the present—only focusing on what is happening in your body in the now. By making it a practice, you will gain better control over your thoughts and heighten your ability to appreciate the present.

Practical Steps To Peace: Remain Mindful (Most Times)

1. Pay attention to the thoughts that cloud your mind daily. Identify how the thoughts that you have make you feel.
2. Identify the patterns. What thoughts make you feel a specific way?
3. Make a list of your triggers.
4. Challenge the thoughts that come up. Ask yourself about the evidence that the thought you are having is true? Evidence that it is false? How can you be certain that its true or false? And what alternatives can you make use of?
5. Practice deep breathing and going into a mental safe place to calm your mind and body.
6. Recognize and accept that you are in greater control than you have previously thought.
7. Identify one behavior that you can do that reminds you that this is your life.

"To me, every hour of the light and dark is a miracle. Every cubic inch of space is a miracle."

—Walt Whitman

13

Leave space for miracles.

It's great to have a plan but the majority of amazing things that happen for us are outside of our control and we couldn't plan it if we tried.

Do you believe in miracles? To me a miracle is anything that happens that you didn't plan. That may be a watered down version of miracle but this is the simplest and most relatable idea of miracle that works for my clients and I. I believe that a vast majority of what happens in life is due to miracles, although we often tend to take credit for what happens. There is a famous adage that luck is 90% preparation and 10% opportunity. I believe that there is a big percentage of that that falls in the miracle category. Sometimes things happen for us in spite of all the things that we have planned. We take such great pains to plan everything perfectly. We stress for hours on end, worrying about what others think, how things will turn and what to do if they don't go well. What life has taught me is that when things don't go well there is always something better around the corner. This idea can seem confusing because sometimes that next thing doesn't look much better and it comes with its own set of problems. But adopting this perspective invites you to play the long game.

I have an analogy that I share with clients. Imagine life as a puzzle--a giant puzzle and all your experiences are puzzle pieces that fit together to form the picture on the box. As you go through life, some of the experiences that you have stand out clearly as anchors (or corner pieces). You know exactly what they mean and where they fit. But with the vast number of experiences we have, most of these pieces are not clear. We are not sure exactly where they fit. It is not until we collect enough pieces that we are able to see the bigger picture and exactly where they fit. Sometimes we have that odd piece that just does not seem to fit. We can't even imagine that its part of the actual puzzle--we may even think it's an extra piece. And it is not until the very end that we are able to place it.

This analogy comes in handy when a client is stuck and trying their hardest to understand a particularly difficult experience. We often pursue understanding with such fervor that we lose all perspective and the understanding becomes the destination instead of the journey. Being open to the idea that some pieces of the puzzle cannot be known by searching at this point in time, it releases us from the endless search and find that holds some of us hostage.

What is most important about this is the idea that our experiences are not cookie-cutter and predictable. They happen in a random way that discretely fit together over time. THis is not an indication that we should just throw our hands up and do nothing instead, it is a reminder to plan well but leave space for the random configuration of good things that make what we aspire to, not only possible but probably. When we overplan, we squeeze out the spontaneous miracle and the miracles have to find their way in by disturbing the flow of what we have planned. Oftentimes we see it as a disturbance--disappointing us, instead of the godsends that they are.

The Braid collective introduced the blackboard method as a tool for manifestation. I believe it is a perfect example of inviting miracles into your life and business. The idea behind the blackboard method is to write down your goals and create space for them to manifest. For example, if one of the company's goals was to work with 12 clients in the quarter, they would write it on the blackboard and draw 12 lines signifying the 12 clients they are expecting. As the clients come in, their names get written in the lines until all the spaces are filled. This may seem like some woo-woo bit, but if we understand that the universe likes to fill empty spaces, we will understand that creating space for things to happen is as plausible as planning for them to happen.

Habit To Peace: Visioning and Future-Self Journaling

Create a space in your life where you write down the things that you are expecting to show up for you. Some people have a vision board (a pictorial representation of their hopes and dreams but it can be as simple as a sheet of paper. One thing to consider is that writing it down is only one piece, creating the space in your life for miracles to show up is another piece of the puzzle.

Practical Steps to Peace: (Adapted from Dr. Nicole PeRera's Future Self Journaling worksheet)

- Step 1: Choosing which behavior to work on
  The first step is to decide on the behavior that you want to change. Using a fresh sheet of paper or notebook, ask yourself the following questions
  - What behavior or pattern do I want to change? Choose one behavior that you want to actively work on changing or developing. If you're struggling to figure this out, try to think about which behavior would make the biggest impact in your life if you managed to change or cultivate it.
  - Which affirmations will help me achieve this? Write down any affirmations you come up with that will help inspire you as you work on the behavior you've chosen.
  - How can I practice this new behavior in my daily life?
- Step 2: Journaling towards your future self

Once the preparatory step is done, we can move onto the journaling practice itself. It's fairly straightforward – we simply write down the following 6 things every day for the next 30 days:

1. My daily affirmation... (e.g. My actions represent the person I am becoming.)

2. Today I will focus on shifting my pattern of...(e.g. ... prioritizing actions that gratify my present self over actions that serve my future self.)

3. I am grateful for... (e.g. ... the possibility to create my own schedule, my significant other, and access to free yoga on YouTube.)

4. The person I'm becoming will experience more...(:e.g. ... self-growth, resilience and alignment.)

5. I have an opportunity to be my future self today when I...(e.g. meditate, prepare a healthy meal and take action on my goals.)

6. When I think about who I'm becoming I feel... (e.g...confident and motivated to take action.)

"You must have the courage to trust your instincts and be ready to question what other people don't. If you do that, you can seize opportunities that others would miss. Believe in yourself, and use everything you can - including the obstacles - to propel you along the road to success. Who knows what you might achieve?"

—Richard Branson

14

Trust your instincts.

When we've made a lot of wrong decisions in the past or chosen things and people that have caused us great harm, we lose the ability to trust our gut. From a cognitive perspective we begin to believe that if we've been so wrong in the past that we cannot trust ourselves. And to a large extent, when we let ourselves down, we begin to lose faith in our abilities to make solid choices that benefit us. But we were all born with innate guidance and wisdom that are meant to help us navigate this journey. If you have been living without trusting your gut, it may take a while to recalibrate but you can reset it.

Trusting yourself is a practice. It is like a muscle that grows over time as you build it. It's important to realize that you can't develop a practice if you don't start somewhere. How is it that you learn to trust anyone in your life? Paying attention to their words and their actions and ensuring that they line up. Measuring their consistency. And ultimately having faith that they are who they have proven themselves to be. Well the last part is a little easier, because you are sure that you are who you say you are or, at least, who you intend to be. You just need to work on being consistent with yourself and ensuring that your words and deeds match more often than not.

Learning to be consistent with yourself, starts with a commitment to you. The commitment asks that you take a risk on you. That you realize that you are worthy of your own time and effort and because you are so important, that you will do all that you can to prove it. The next step is to actually show up for yourself. To say the hard things you need to say. To enforce the boundaries when someone breaches them. To take the time to rest when you feel overwhelmed and your body is calling for rest. The more consistent and responsive you are to yourself the more your mind and heart learns that they can trust you. The more they learn they can trust you, the

When you do, trust your gut. It is NEVER wrong.

When you feel in your gut that it's time to leave, stop or do something, do it. It doesn't have to make sense, don't wait to find out why. Oftentimes you end up with a lot of wasted time and regrets.

Habit to Peace: Practice Strengthening Your Intuition

Spend a few minutes every day listening to your internal dialogue and asking yourself questions about what you should do next. Pay attention to any promptings that you have to do something. Sometimes it's a small voice. Pay attention to what happens after you hear the voice and how your body feels when you are being guided.

Practical Steps To Peace: Listen To and Strengthen Your Intuition:

1. Stop and listen to your inner voice. Take a deep breath and give yourself a little space between what you think and what you do. In that moment, ask yourself what to do and listen to your inner voice.
2. Act on your instinctual inclinations. Take note of what you were led to do. What are the outcomes? Is there any evidence to support that this was the right decision? How do you feel after having made this decision?
3. Review. What lessons did you learn from this decision? How could things have been different had you taken a different path? Were there any signs to indicate that you had made the wrong or right decision? How long did it take you to feel at peace?

When you continue to make decisions considering your internal guidance system, the stronger it becomes and the more accurate and in alignment your decisions will be.

"You are magnificent beyond measure, perfect in your imperfections, and wonderfully made."

— Abiola Abrams

15

Finished is better than perfect.

Perfectionism is by far one of the things that keeps people stuck and unable to move forward to achieve the life they want. Start and finish something. It doesn't have to be perfect, it just has to be finished. You can work on perfecting it after it's been published, defended or submitted.

Do you have an idea for a business, program, book, project that you want to do but can't get started? 9 times out of 10, you're where you are because you're overthinking it and wanting it to be perfect.

We live in a world where every television commercial sells us the idea of perfection--from perfect beauty, to perfect bodies, to perfect homes. We are constantly reminded that we are imperfect and if we only buy this new thingamajig then we will be like all the other perfect people in the world. Cue buzzer sound. That is a lie and we may have covered this but nobody's perfect. No one's life looks like the perfection you see and striving to fit into the false culture of perfection only wears you down.

Some of us take pride in being called perfectionists because, for some reason, it means that we have a higher standard than everyone else. But if we were to truly be honest and ask how perfection serves us, we'd find that it increases our anxiety, creates unnecessary stress and holds us back from accomplishing a myriad of things we would like to accomplish. Perfectionism is not a virtue. Taking pride in your work or presentation is--ensuring that you present high quality work that you're proud of is a good reframe, but anytime we casually miss in the idea of perfection, we're setting ourselves up for unnecessary stress.

For me, perfectionism can look like endlessly researching a topic that I know back and forth to see that other people also feel the same way (let's call it perfectionism with a side of need for validation, but hey, it is what it is). It also looks like not starting a project until I have the perfect idea, perfect design, perfect way to market or perfect everything. In order to start, it actually has to be finished in my mind. That has stopped me from writing 19 books, publishing 3 journals, running 12 retreats and just being awesome. The worry behind this form of insecurity is that it will misrepresent your awesomeness if it is not perfect, but the big secret is that nobody's work is perfect. And only you will know that it wasn't as perfect as you'd hope. I love Paulo Coelho's work and I'm sure he doesn't think his work is perfect. Well actually, there's a name for people who think their work is perfect and it's not a pretty one.

In addition, we get stuck in the belief that if we put something out that it's gone forever and there's nothing that we can do to change it. The truth is that while there are tons of first and only editions, that is a personal choice. Things can always be edited, updated, revised and retracted. You can do a version 2, a revised edition, a replacement or just scrap it and start over.

One major disadvantage of remaining in perfectionism is that your self esteem can take a hit because once you delay making progress on a goal or completing it at all, you start to doubt yourself--about whether or not you can even do it. And if you feed yourself that message enough times, your perfectionism turns into self doubt and fear. Finishing something reinforces your mind's belief that you can get things done. It doesn't matter how it's done really. Confidence is built after repetition. The more you do it, the more confident you are that you can do it.

Habit To Peace: Release The Need for Perfect as the Only Metric

Do something toward your goal everyday. Get into the habit of writing, tinkering, creating something and at the end of a set time period, use the ones you love and put away the ones you don't. Creating a habit will change your attachment to something being perfect. When perfect is not the only metric for progress you can create freely without being anchored down by an undefinable goal. Aim for enjoyment. Aim for growth. Aim for learning. Challenge yourself and welcome the beginner's mind again.

Challenge yourself to do something that is not perfect, purely for fun.

Practical Steps to Peace: Get Things Done (Imperfectly):

1. Let go of the belief that the first one has to be the best and only one. Play around with the idea that whatever you're doing is just a test that you can go back and tweak after you get the results. Release your poor self esteem from being held captive by the perfection in your work. We are growing beings with growing ideas. So the meaning of your whole life doesn't have to be tied to this one idea.

2. Give yourself permission to have multiple editions. Make clear to yourself that this is the first go and it's okay to be bad. In fact, allow crap to be a part of your process. So first go should be crap and allow it to be as crappy as it can be. Then build in a second edition and maybe allow the third to be seen by someone else. It's more important to get working and churn something out than to be stuck in productivity purgatory where there's a whole lot of fire and pressure and very little actually getting done.

3. Get an accountability buddy (free or paid) that will help you stay on track and ask to see evidence of your progress.

4. Create a sign above our desk or wherever you work that says "Progress is better than Perfection" or "Done is better than perfect." I continuously chanted "done is better than perfect" in order to get my dissertation done and I was in total fear that I would fail it. SO if it can work for me, it can definitely work for you.

5. Set deadlines to get it done and have a consequence attached to not meeting that deadline. This helps to minimize the need for perfection because perfectionists prefer to deliver than have nothing at all.

"There will never come a time when we are complete and finished human beings because the state of being complete and finished is the antithesis of what being human is all about."

16

Life is a work in progress.

There was a time when I had a huge list with dates and times that I wanted to accomplish life by. As time passed by and I gained more life experience, I realized that I had placed so many unrealistic expectations on myself. No wonder I was always feeling so behind everyone and everything else. I expected that once I accomplished the things on my list, life could begin or I expected that I would then be happy. What I know now is that I never really understood life and that there is no clear end point (well, death).

The concept of being human doesn't allow for things to ever be complete. As long as there is life there is movement and change. Even if we don't want it, we are always in flux. There is no perfect place to get to. There is no finished. Things can always get better, they can always change. I'm sorry you have to hear this from me but this idea of perfection that we're aiming for, that is keeping you stuck and afraid to act does not exist. Everything is a work in progress.

This should give you some relief because if everything is a work in progress, you are free to make mistakes in pursuit of knowledge and growth. If everything is a work in progress, you can accept yourself as you are and keep working on the things you want to do and become. If everything is a work in progress, we are really always becoming and there's no need to get there NOW!

One of the lessons that I had to learn to help me get closer to peace was that life as a work in progress means that the rush to get where someone else already got to is really unnecessary. I think that understanding the concept of life as a work helps to remember that it is something that we need to continuously be working at. Living life, being more present in life, recalibrating our understanding and experiencing of life is something we have to be intentional about. It won't happen on its own and it won't happen without our intervention. The In-progress portion of the saying is a reminder that life does not stop moving even when we choose to do nothing. The days are still going, the years are still passing by whether we choose to be active participants in our lives or not. We will get older. Life will progress. It is fully up to each and every one of us how we participate in that. We are either active participants working hand in hand with life or we are passive recipients of whatever comes.

And if life is a work in progress then my responsibility is to do the work.

The Japanese have a term known as Kaizen that can help us on our quest for seeing life as a work in progress. Kaizen refers to continuous improvement. Like its friend, lifelong learning, continuous improvement is a principle that yields ten-fold returns. The nuanced meaning of the word Kaizen is that the improvements are tiny, which means that there is no expectation that tomorrow you'll make a massive change and everything will be different. In fact, it is intentional, small changes, sometimes almost too small to identify, but the consciousness of the changes result in a large change at the end. Kaizen applied to loving yourself means, dropping the sudden sprints to get to the end and replacing them with measured steps taken consistently.

Habit to Peace: Release yourself daily from the expectation that you are supposed to be perfect.

When we carry around the expectation that we are supposed to be an undefined representation of perfection, we hold ourselves hostage and make our lives images of disappointment. We become paradigms of disappointment. The practice of releasing perfection is a simple one that builds our sense of self worth over time. At first it might be challenging to do because we'd held disappointment in ourselves as a close friend for so long. At first our brains and our hearts may resist and it will feel difficult but with continued practice, our minds and hearts will soften to the concept.

Practical Steps to Peace:

1. Write a list of ways that you are already good enough as you are. Writing this list helps you to identify that there are parts of you that do not need changing. No one ever needs a complete overhaul of all their habits. Taking inventory of what are the good things that can stay lays the foundation for all change. Now these parts can get better but let's start by identifying the good.

2. Write a list of ways that you want to continue changing and growing. This practice allows us to remember that nothing is stagnant. If you approach this exercise understanding that growth in the direction you want to go requires intention, then identifying areas of growth and change without judgment makes this a positive exercise. Too often, when we identify areas that need to change, our desire comes from a place of dissatisfaction and criticism. Release the need to be critical and visualize what changes in these areas could look like for your life.

3. Write a list of the strengths and skills that you need to embrace more or new skills you need to develop. This tops the cake. Where else would you like to develop and what are the things that can help you get there?

"Your children are not your children. They are the sons and daughters of Life's longing for itself. They come through you but not from you, And though they are with you yet they belong not to you."

—Kahlil Gibran

17

You do not own your children (or anyone for that matter).

You are your children's guides through the world. Everybody has their own individual purpose and destiny. You were chosen to help their souls to the point where they can make their own decisions. Nurture them. Identify and build their strengths. Help them live their lives. Help them to love learning whatever they love. Try to do more good than harm, because you will always do some harm. Don't be deterred.

Much damage has been done in the name of ownership or in the attempt to own. Let's start with slavery. Some of the negative effects of slavery stemmed from the stringent methods that were administered to remind the slaves that they were property and were not entitled to their own...their own lives, their own families, their own land. While parenting isn't necessarily comparable to slavery, some parents forget that it is not slavery.

One of the things I have come face to face with as a parent is the fact that my child is a whole person by herself. She listens to me because she likes me and doesn't want to get in trouble but given the opportunity, she does what she wants. And often what she wants to do isn't what I want her to do. I have had to quickly release my preconceived notions of what it means to be an effective parent and redefine for myself based on who my child is, what an effective parent, for her, looks like.

My current position has been informed by Dr. Shefali Tsabary and her work on conscious parenting and honestly, sometimes, I struggle.

I grew up fearing my parents and doing what they wanted (for the most part) because I don't want to get a beating. And sometimes, I braved the beating anyway, because my motivation to get what I wanted was stronger than any threat or actual whooping.

Many of us would have had a deeper understanding of life if our parents mentored us instead of trying to drive the fear of them into us. I understand as a parent that we only want the best for our kids. No relatively reasonable and emotionally intact parent wants harm to come to their child. In fact, many parents will go above and beyond what is normative to help their child (we all know the outcomes of this). Yet, they fail to understand that their child has their unique perspective and unique desires and by being a guide for them, they are able to steer them more successfully in the direction that is likely to benefit their child.

This same issue is often resonant in adult relationships with parents, siblings and romantic partners. We have mistakenly come to believe that because they have chosen to partner with us through life that means that they have some obligation to live life as we have determined is well and good for them.

Habits to Peace: Accepting Others as Independent

See your child and others as independent beings on their own journeys through life. Operate accordingly.

Practical Steps to Peace: Accept Yourself as Independent of Others Too

1. Ask the loved ones in your life about their dreams and desires. Practice active listening as you complete this exercise, suspending your judgments about their responses and offering support and encouragement. Take note of what you hear.
2. Evaluate in your mind the alignment between what they desire for themselves and their personalities?
3. Question the origins of your desires for the other. Where did it come from? Are these desires a reflection of you or of them?

"You have no responsibility to live up to what other people think you ought to accomplish. I have no responsibility to be like they expect me to be. It's their mistake, not my failing."

— Richard P. Feynman

18

Don't believe what everyone else tells you is important.

No matter if people have done the same thing for 40 years, you don't have to do them. Ask good questions and make decisions that are best for you. Some things worked in an earlier time and no longer work now (see cassette player for an example).

How many truly happy, intentional, on-purpose people do you know? And how many of them are actually giving you advice? What I have found over the years is that people who are happy and on purpose have very little time to be giving you advice on your life. And if they do give you some advice, it is measured and peppered with examples of why this may not particularly apply to your life.

History has shown that no single decision results in the same outcome for everyone. That is why no two people have the exact journey to wealth and happiness. No two people have the same fitness or love journey. This is because everyone is different and everyone's perspective and life choices will yield different results in their lives.

It's important, however, to remember that everyone is still trying to figure it out. Not even the dead have it all figured out. Wouldn't it be nice if you died when you've gotten all the answers and your life was going perfectly. More likely than not the people who have died in peace, have made peace with themselves and their life circumstances. It hasn't been because of perfect circumstances.

Anyone, including me, can only advise you to the best of my experience and knowledge and sometimes intuition. I cannot predict anyone else's life and their outcomes. And you shouldn't take anyone else's advice as gospel. Be open to the idea that they may know a little more than you do on a particular subject or have more experience than you but it doesn't mean that their advice on your life will end well or be good for you. And no matter how many years someone has been doing something, it doesn't mean that is the only right way to do it and that no new ways can be invented. I want to add a caveat because I believe in not reinventing the wheel and a lot of good time tested advice has value. It doesn't mean to just swallow it up as gospel. What I am suggesting is critical analysis and evaluation of what you are being presented with and deciding whether or not it is a good fit for you in your present circumstance. Give an ear without taking it as your path.

Ultimately your path will be a result of trial and error. The people who have stuck to one consistent path without deviation or questioning, end up miserable.

Habit To Peace: Keep a Curious Approach to Your Own Thoughts

Ask yourself questions about the ways that you think and the decisions you are choosing to make. Self knowledge is self development's first law. A purposeful journey into understanding yourself and what is deeply important to you, despite what society or anyone else tells you will help you get closer to your own self satisfaction.

Practical Steps to Peace: Maintaining Curiosity

1. Release the need to judge your thoughts. There's a common quoted idea that may help- your feelings are not facts. In fact, your feelings are the opposite of facts. Examine them with a light curiosity. And then release them.
2. Journal around the beliefs and ideas that you hold. Where did they come from? How did you develop them? What's important to you and why? If you had ro release these "important things" what would change about your life?

3. For a day or two, pay attention to the things that you actually do in your day to day life. How often are the things that you have identified as important showing up for you? How do you feel about them when they actually do show up?

4. Make adjustments to ensure that the important things that bring you a sense of fulfillment have a recurring role in your life whether you need to schedule them in or set aside a block of time to cultivate them.

"A society grows great when old men plant trees whose shade they know they shall never sit in."

19

Make every place you leave a little bit better than you found it.

I try my best to do this and hope that I have succeeded. The easiest way to do this is through making other people feel seen and heard.

Every one of us has dreams. Some of us harbor big aspirations of changing the world. We believe that we are filled with the potential for greatness,.. And if we don't achieve that big dream then our lives have been wasted. I have been there, shaking with fear that I may never do the BIG things that I want and how disappointed I will be with myself.

It's funny because every day, I get in a session with a client and help themselves their worth, choose themselves, and heal from the damage of the past. I am making a difference and every minute that

I sit with someone who needs an ear, I am making the world a little better.

We may not have much opportunity everyday to make a life changing impact on the world but we do have the opportunity to create a tiny impact in every place or person that we meet. Because of the focus on celebrity we have come to believe that only big acts make waves. And if it isn't plastered all over social media and the news then we don't matter.

One of the most influential people I have met in my life and someone I aim to be like is my mentor in college. She was compassionate and caring and single-handedly rescued me and my self-esteem. When you were in her presence, you felt seen and heard. And the times I didn't have that I have yearned for it. And she has that way with everyone. She may not win the Nobel Peace prize or become Kardashian famous, but there are countless people, like myself, walking around with her stamp of goodness on them.

See, many people are suffering in search of their big thing--that thing that makes people know our names and greet us well, yet we walk by opportunities to make lasting and significant impact when we ignore people who could do well with a smile, an uplifting word, a few minutes in conversation about the things that matter to them. We don't even acknowledge these as opportunities for significance. Sometimes, we see them as bothers. If we can just shift our perspective a little, we can pepper our lives with many moments of magic-making for ourselves and others. If we take up the mantle to make every place and person that we encounter better than we found them, we will have acquired a lifetime of significance far more meaningful.

Habit To Peace: Walk into every situation with a purpose for your presence

Pay attention to the purpose that you hold in every interaction with a person or place you encounter. While it may be challenging at times due to our fast paced lives, developing the habit of assigning purpose to your presence will increase your understanding of your value. You will also be more attuned to the value that you bring into a space. Being deliberate about our time and energy and intentionally co-creating with the world and people around us deepens the meaning that we find in life.

Practical Steps to Peace: Maintaining Purposeful Presence

1. Be intentional about leaving things better than you found them. If this is your intention, you will hold an awareness of the things that could be better or at least that you are not causing harm.

2. Engage with the space or person with a sense of care and sacredness. Treating someone with care inherently increases the value of the interaction. Similarly, treating a space with care increases the value of your actions.

3. Ask yourself frequently, "Am I adding value to this person's life or to this space that I am inhabiting?" Reassess frequently and adjust your actions accordingly.

"The path from dreams to success does exist. May you have the vision to find it, the courage to get on to it, and the perseverance to follow it."

—Kalpana Chawla

20

Always have a vision for your life.

It may never work out exactly as you envision, but it will be a compass for you, guiding you toward something.

Can you remember the feeling of being in the place when you have just made it out alive of a situation that you thought you would never survive? You have the feeling that you're in the clear but you're not really sure where to go and what to do next or even if you want to do anything next. The temptation is to sit there and just breathe through it. You are so happy that you made it, that it could be so difficult to envision being anywhere else. And sometimes it is the fear of moving forward and facing the same or similar challenge that can keep you stuck in the same spot. Yet, because you understand that life moves forward, whether you want it to or not, it is imperative that you make a conscious choice to move from there forward.

If you've had a difficult life, where you have come face to face with challenges time after time, with nothing working out for you the way you thought it would, it's challenging to try to envision a future working out differently. Most people with trauma histories will tell you that they have never envisioned their lives past a certain point because they couldn't see past the pain to a life in which they would prosper. It seems counterintuitive, yet a vision for your future is exactly what you need to create a future that is different from the past.

Holding a solid vision for the future is one of the key ways to begin the process of moving forward into a different life. I am not suggesting living in a fantasy world divorced from reality. Instead, I am advocating creating a map of sorts. I believe that there is a process through which change occurs. Because the universe is ordered, all change happens in a progressive way. Nothing is happenstance.

The Thrive Process of Change (My not-so-unique change framework) posits that in order to move from one place to the next you:

1. Acknowledge where you are. Before any change can happen, you have to be willing to own the spot on which you stand. Where are you exactly? What is happening here? If you are

unable to acknowledge what has happened it will be very difficult to move forward.

2. Accept where you are and the reasons that you are there. This is not asking you to be okay with where you are, just to accept that you are in this place and there are reasons why you are here. Once you are able to do that, then it becomes easier to move forward because not only will you know from where you're moving, you'll have awareness about what got you there, kept you there and need to let go of to move from there.

3. Identify where you need to go so that you can then mobilize the resources that you need to get there. Remember that humans are innately resilient. The journey of life is by nature harrowing. Yet, we survive. Yet we rise and thrive. As humans, we have an extraordinary capacity--that of adapting easily. Unfortunately, sometimes we are forced to adapt to painful and difficult situations. But this capacity doesn't only apply to difficult situations, we have the ability to adapt to peaceful and calm situations as well.

The challenge after a difficult series of situation is to rise and live deeper, more meaningful lives. Dr. Viktor Frankl (Man's Search for Meaning), observed that prisoners who had lost their faith in the future lost their "spiritual hold on themselves, and quickly declined mentally and physically." This indicates that a hope in some future is important for humans to maintain their sense of wellness. This is why having a vision is essential; however, not only having a vision but actively holding and working towards the vision is important for the change process.

Giving your brain something to aspire to in the face of challenge can keep you grounded. A common complaint seen in people who have lost their vision, is feeling lost, and purposeless. The desperation that they face is palpable. In their eyes it brings up existential questions--why am I even here? What is all of this for? And while questioning is encouraged (you should question), questioning without purpose is a futile effort and only adds to the feeling of desolation.

When I speak of vision, I mean a relatively clear picture of where you want to go and what you want it to feel like. Some people create vision boards to serve as a visual representation, some people have verbal affirmations, others hold a picture in their minds. I am not partial to any format. What is important is that you have one that you are routinely honing.

Habit to Peace: Hold the Vision of Your Future Self in your Mind Daily

Ask yourself daily how you can be a bit more like your future self today. Write down your big wins and the things that you learned at the end of each day. Being focused on the vision that you have for yourself and your life and checking in regularly with yourself keeps you committed to the path that you have crafted for yourself.

Practical steps to Peace: Drafting Your Future Self

1. Get a notebook or a few sheets of paper. Take a few minutes to relax yourself. Close your eyes and imagine your life in the future as you would want it to be. Really sink into the movie of your life. What do you want your life to look like in 1 year or 5 years from now? What do you want your life to feel like? Where do you want to be? Who do you want to be with? What are you doing? What do you want your family to look like? What would you like your career to be? Picture it and see it in as vivid detail as you can.

2. When you have sat with the video and know how it feels in your body. Think of a one sentence statement that summarizes your vision. Write it down and put it somewhere you can see it. Then write down three to five things that you can do to move you closer to the life that you envisioned. These are the things that you will focus on in the next couple of months that will bring you closer to reaching your vision.

3. Be flexible. Be open to the fact that your current version of the vision will need to be changed as time goes by and you have become more comfortable, more at peace and circumstances change. I want you to think of your current version of your vision as a living breathing thing that is supposed to change. It, like you, is a work in progress.

"Some things benefit from shocks; they thrive and grow when exposed to volatility, randomness, disorder, and stressors and love adventure, risk, and uncertainty."

— Nassim Nicholas Taleb, Antifragile

21

You will survive.

This lesson has been the most up to date I have learned. If you were to have a peek into my life you would see that ALL my life I have struggled with relationships and the desire to belong. It has driven me to humiliate, beg, angry fits of rage and unbearable silence. While I know relationships are one of the most important facets of the human experience, they have been a painful part of my life.

I grew up feeling unloved and unwanted. I know that there are members of my family that truly love me--whether they are able to show it or not and most likely because I wasn't able to receive it. But the bottom line is that the people who I believed were supposed to love me best, have been unable to for whatever reasons. And for more years than I can remember, I have fervently sought their love and approval. Looking back on my life, I have always defined myself as a "relationship person" constantly in search of love and family. Neither of which has come easily.

What that has looked like for me is feeling utterly alone and dejected, with a growing resentment for the people who have shown up poorly in my life. I think a large part of it was that it placed emphasis on their existence in my life as a necessary condition for happiness. And so when things didn't turn out as I planned, I couldn't see my way through to happiness. Over time, as I have grown and realized the extent of everyone's challenges to find their own place in the world, I have grown to accept that I am mine and mine alone and no matter what life throws at me, I will survive. As long as I choose to keep going, with a cheerful heart and hope and a dash of optimism, I will be here.

This particular mindset has resulted in a kind of self-ownership that I didn't know possible. It has helped me to take the good with the bad and edit my life as needed. It has provided me with a secure place to land because no matter what happens, I will always have myself. And I will always do my best for myself.

Closely tied to the idea that you will survive is the idea that this is your life and you really only have full responsibility for yourself. Even if you have good friends who choose to show up for you, you have a duty and obligation to show up FULLY for yourself. YOU owe yourself that much. And no one owes you that, not even your children. You are the only one responsible for you and as long as you are fully aware of that, it guides your decisions. It frees you to go and live the life that you want to live. To go to the places that you want to go, to not sit around and wait for someone to choose me, to begin the creation of the experience that you want to have and not have it be dependent on anyone else to be there, to confirm, to contribute to or to support you. This makes any input from another a blessing as opposed to an obligation. And from a perspective of full ownership, you will be able to appreciate it with glee.

One simple phrase that can help you to throw away any bad moments when they push their heads up is "keep going." While it is important to have a direction, it is more important that while going in that direction, should you get tired or worried or feel like quitting to just put your head down and go. It doesn't matter the pace. One step at a time.

I use this strategy in my workouts. I HATE jogging for long distances. I am a sprinter. But when I have to jog, I place my eyes on the ground, and move my legs. I know that as long as I keep moving I will finish. I know that one foot in front of the other will get me there. I know and I repeat over and over to myself as I run that "there's nothing to it but to do it." Repeating this phrase grounds me. It helps me get out of my head and into my body. It helps me to keep going even when my mind tells me to stop because I'm tired. It makes the act of getting done more concrete for me.

I came across a phrase that perfectly sums up this idea. It is known as Anti-fragile and there's a whole book written about it. The idea behind antifragility is that as humans we have the capability to flex when life throws stuff at us. We essentially take the hit and use it to build our next steps. Instead of getting deterred; we take it and keep rolling right along. If I could marry the phrase antifragile, I would. I am anti-fragile and anti-fragile is me. If nothing else, my life has shown me that I am one tough girl. I am by definition- antifragile because life has dealt with me roughly and I have taken the punches and kept on rolling.

Adopting the anti-fragile mindset has actually changed my life. It underscored the innate resilience in myself and all other humans. We can, do and will survive. We're made for it. I want to remind you that no matter what life looks like at this point in time. You will survive. And if you commit to the idea that you will survive despite the obstacles and the odds, it can take the sting out of the things that don't go so well.

Habit To Peace: Affirm Yourself Often

Use positive affirmations that affirm the traits that you want to strengthen or to develop in your life. While they may seem fake at first, repeating them with conviction and looking for ways to prove their possibility in your life will hasten their manifestation.

Practical Steps to Peace: Use Affirmations That Strengthen

1. Create a personal mantra that affirms your commitment to you being the total owner of your life experience. Remind yourself that you will survive.

2. Print it out, put it in your mirror, in your bag, on your computer, on your phone--anywhere and everywhere that you can see it and be reminded that you are a total badass, with a double layer of anti-fragility and a complete life ownership superpower. Life can throw anything at you but you get right back up and stare it in the face. You got this.

3. Create a Playlist of songs or verbal affirmations of the traits that you want to display and your commitment to being the person who displays those traits. Listen to it daily. Not only will you soak it up but it will encourage you slowly to live into those traits.

"Nourishing yourself in a way that helps you blossom in the direction you want to go is attainable, and you are worth the effort."

Deborah Day

22

Self care is a necessity.

When survivors survive, their natural instinct isn't to rest and rejuvenate. It is to continue to push and to go even harder often to make up for what they lost or was taken from them. Think of it as a driving force to never, ever be in the same place again. I find that survivors often push for growth at the expense of their mental and emotional well-being and over time, they learn to not take care of themselves.

On the journey of healing and development, self care is one of the pillars. It may seem counterintuitive but like in the sport of weightlifting and bodybuilding, in order for the muscle you just stretched and manipulated to grow, it needs to rest. In order for us to extract all that we can from our growth and healing journeys, we need to nurture and nourish our bodies, spirits and minds. There are a number of pillars of self care: emotional, social, psychological, mental and spiritual.

There are lots of ways to take care of yourself, most completely subjective. There is some common understanding about what comprises good self care. So, if humans came with manual, here are a few tips that might be in the care guide:

1. Get the sleep you need. This isn't the same for everyone, but most adult humans thrive best on between seven and nine hours.

2. Eat healthy. There is a strong food-mood connection. In fact, there is even a whole branch of psychiatry devoted to nutrition (Nutritional Psychiatry). Some of the best mood boosting foods are ginger, turmeric, fish, chia, flax, berries (colors, every color is an antioxidant), green tea, mushrooms, avocados, and broccoli.

3. Meditate. Meditation helps build mental and emotional resilience and can help to manage anxiety.

4. Spend some time in nature. Research shows that visits to gardens, rural areas, and other green areas can improve thinking skills and reduce stress.

5. Immerse yourself in a good book. Reading fiction improves brain and social functioning and boosts empathy.

6. Say yes...and no. People who are open to new experiences literally see the world differently according to research. But, setting boundaries on your time is also essential to well-

being. It's important to realize that saying no gives you space to say yes to new opportunities and experiences.

7. Make time for friends and other social support. Close relationships have a wide range of benefits: they motivate us, inform us, help us grow. And, they also have substantial mental health benefits. In fact, not having close friends is a risk factor for both anxiety and depression.

8. Get to know yourself better. Part of caring for yourself is doing things that are important to you. It's easy to get so caught up in what other people are doing or what we think we should be doing, that we lose sight of what's actually important to us.

9. Take a social media break. Scrolling through Instagram feels like a fun indulgence, but it's the nutritional equivalent of eating a big bag of chips: satisfying in the moment, addicting, and leaves you feeling remorseful and maybe a little sick. It also can make you lonely, which has legitimate health consequences.

10. Daydream, often. Letting your mind wander is linked to intelligence and mental health. And, it doesn't matter what you're daydreaming about. So, don't feel guilty, embrace it!

Habit to Peace: Make Self Care One of the Pillars in Your Life

Define self care as a bucket in your life that needs to be filled, quite like any other major area of your life e.g. career, fun, family and friends, spirituality. Allocate space in your calendar and budget to complete practices that encompass self care. Remember that there are different layers of self care. There's maintenance self care for when the skin are going well. These may be the bubble baths and face masks. Then there is Crisis Care for when you're in the middle of turmoil, chaos or trauma. This is a deeper, more soul level care and requires a commitment to nurturing and Nourishing the hurt parts of you. Then there is recovery self care which is still very delicate and intentional but may also include lighter aspects of self care. Allowing yourself to experience deep dark feelings and allowing yourself to sit In them is a way to shore up your resources. This too is self care.

Practical Steps to Peace: Define Your Self Care Layers

1. Identify the habits and behaviors that leave you feeling rejuvenated after completing them. Keep a running list in the back of your planner.

2. Identify the different layers of self care that you may need as well as the times that you may need them. Your authentic self care experiences are solely yours. They don't have to appeal to anyone else. They just have to nurture, nourish and replenish you.

3. When you are planning your week or month, schedule at least one of each activity per week, based on the time that you are in.

23

Who you are being is way more important than what you are doing

One of the most healing shifts anyone can make along their life journey is to turn the lens with which they view life and themselves inward instead of looking outward. That means, shifting from looking for external validation, external support, external meaning and purpose to one that is defined by your internal morals, values and self definition. Thus requires you to focus more on who you are being in the world instead of who others are being to you, from what you are doing in the world to who is the person you want to be as you do things. The changes you will experience as a result will change your entire path.

For most of our lives we learned that the input of others, parents, friends, teachers, mentors, gurus and everyone else we perceived to have value was more important than what we thought and who we were. We often strive to be a version of them or who they deemed to be acceptable. Some of us are still striving to please our parents and be who they thought we should be. Yet in order for us to live full lives, we have to come to the realization and understanding that we are best served by being clear on who we want to be in the world and living from that space. We have infinite potential. And though experiences may have beaten us down to where we doubt our ability to translate bad experiences into gold, we nevertheless do. It is our birthright--to be alchemists. To take the bad and make it good. To take the good and make it great. The possibilities are endless. Who are you being in this moment? Are you being the version of yourself that you feel good about? Are you being the version of yourself that brings you joy? Are you being the version of yourself that is committed to living a healed, whole life or are you being someone who can never be happy? Are you being someone who is a victim to their circumstances? Are you being someone who loves and is love? Or are you someone who is in dire need of love and is living in a state of depression and desperation?

Who you choose to be is a powerful differentiation from who you just assume you are.

Many people believe that who they are is who they have been born to be. The scientific community has proven that who we "are" is the sum of our biological origins and our social encounters. We are thought to be a product of these things only. However, if you've been through emotion or physical hell and have lived to tell the story, you know that this is only part of the story as there would have been times when you would have willed yourself into joy and peace, when you have coached yourself back from the brim, when you've reached deep within and pulled out the last sliver of hope and used it to spin a good day or week. There is an innate force within you that you can call on to create. And this is your **Being** –a deep, spiritual part of you that makes miracles. Some call it your soul, some call it your highest self. Some call it the God in you.

How would life be if you were to live life from that space?

One of my Mentors, Steve Hardison, *the Ultimate Coach* has a newly released book that he refers to as the book of Being. It challenges you to declare who you choose to be in your life. It asks you to sit with yourself and define the person that you want to be and to create a document declaring who you commit to being. This is a powerful practice because it reminds you daily who you are and who you are committed to being despite what you may encounter. Being is a decision. And by deciding daily, you carve a path in your brain and in your life that serves as a compass for your decisions.

You are challenged to sit with yourself for a few hours to a few days and decide on the person who you want to be. This is the person who you know that you were created to be.

Use this opportunity to release any beliefs or limitations, anything negative that may have been spoken over your life, any beliefs that you acquired about your skills, values or future. This is your opportunity to create for yourself who you will BE from here on out.

As you get clear on who you BE, write your declarations down on a sheet of paper or type it on your phone or computer. This will be known as your document--the thing that holds the sacred definition of your being on paper. You will read this document every day for as long as you live. Your goal is to make this be a living reminder of who you are and how you intend to be in the world.

Habit to Peace: Make Being a Part of Your Self Definition

When we are not clear on who we intend to be in the world, we act from other people's desires. While others' expectations of us can guide our behavior sometimes, optimally we want to be clear about who we are choosing to be and act accordingly. Too often we are motivated by forces that we haven't taken the time to understand and so can be aimless. This aimlessness usually shows up as feelings of being lost and empty. Define yourself by who you choose to BE. That's your highest calling. BE the YOU that you choose to be.

Practical Steps to Peace: Be Clear about Who You Are BEING.

1. Make a list of all the things that you know to be true about you. These things don't have to be validated by anyone else.

Try to identify even the things you consider minor. We're going for truth not ego.

2. Spend some time, as much as you need, creating a list of all the things that you would like to be able to say about yourself. While you complete this exercise, release judgment. You are being asked to create your future and not reevaluate the missteps or mistakes that have happened in the past.

3. Use both lists to create affirmations in the form of I AM about the self that you want to be. Read and continue to edit until your affirmations inspire you. Don't be afraid or discouraged if they don't feel true right now, know that you have infinite potential and these things can and will be true of you.

4. Decide on a time of day that you will repeat your affirmations. Create space in your life physically and mentally for this practice every day and commit to holding this practice for your own healing and growth.

"You are your own worst enemy. If you can learn to stop expecting impossible perfection, in yourself and others, you may find the happiness that has always eluded you."

— Lisa Kleypa

24

Manage your expectations, so you can manage your happiness

If you've found yourself constantly bothered by the behaviors or choices of others, or frequently disappointed by friends, loved ones or others who you've been close to and you may believe that they just do not care as much as you,, you may be right.. However, the problem may not be what you think it is. For many of us, we believe that others just don't care like we do.. they're just lazy or they don't like us. The truth is that we have allowed our expectations to run amok. One of the major challenges that most people who tend to be easily hurt or disappointed face is holding high expectations of others and holding them to their fulfillment. When those expectations are not met, there is an emotional flood that threatens your sanity.

Don't interpret this as a need to have no expectations, instead consider the possibility that others do not value the same things that you value. They don't really care about the things that you deem to be important. They have their own priorities and whatever it is that you expect them to do, may not be their priority.

What would shift for you if you were to release others of the expectations that you hold for them? Especially the ones unbeknownst to them?

What would shift for you, if you just release yourself from monitoring other people's behaviors and value-based on their level of reciprocity?

What would change if you did the things that you wanted to do for yourself and allowed others to do what they wanted to do for themselves and made your decisions accordingly? This may sound like a recipe for disaster as some of the relationships and situations that we are experiencing are solely being held together by our will and extensive effort and we fear that they would fall apart if we stopped. The truth is, they might and likely will. But then what? What would happen next if those one-sided relationships were to fall apart? What would you be free to do? How would you be free to live from then on? What would that mean for your life?

Our expectations keep us shackled to things and people who don't view our needs with the same level of value as we do. That is perfectly acceptable because they have their own priorities. When we place the burden on them to make us happy by falling in line with exactly what we need them to do, our happiness is then determined by their schedule. We rationalize our behaviors and are adamant that things must go the way that we imagine them—because it is the way that we would have done it for them. We make others guilty of betrayal because they didn't or couldn't see our need and we become walking victims. Here's a simple concept that may help to alleviate some of your emotional stress: the longer you hoist others up on a high expectations pole and hold them there with no input from them, the more likely you are to be disappointed and unhappy when those expectations are not met.

So how do you release others from your expectations without feeling bad? You acknowledge the other's humanity and their priorities, understanding that the things they value are significantly more important to them than they are to you and vice versa.

Habit to Peace: Take ownership of your Expectations

Create a mantra to repeat daily that reminds you that you are only responsible for your own behavior and no one else's. It may be something as simple as "Everyone else is responsible for their own behavior." Or "Manage your expectations." Or even "No one has an obligation to meet my expectations. I have the responsibility of managing my emotions."

Practical Steps to Peace:

1. Pay attention to your emotions when you respond to others' behavior. Is your response based on your expectations of them or how you have chosen to respond? Make a deliberate effort to choose to release any negative emotions that you feel surrounding another's behavior. No one owes you a particular behavior. Your responses are yours. Allow them to exist but then release them. Visualize your emotion like a cloud that floats away. Watch as it disappears without holding on. Free yourself.

2. Whenever negative emotions resurface, remind yourself of the mantra that you created to release others from the hook of your expectations.

"Anybody can become angry - that is easy,
but to be angry with the right person and
to the right degree and at the right time
and for the right purpose, and in the right
way - that is not within everybody's power
and is not easy."

— Aristotle

25

Identify, honor and manage your emotions

At any point in time, how connected are you to yourself and your emotions. If you're in survival mode, most of the time the only emotion you are able to process and identify with is anger. In survival, anger is the emotion that drives you to keep going. The brain creates a sense of urgency that anger manifests. It's rare that someone who is in survival mode can experience enthusiasm, or excitement. It is not in their emotional wheelhouse at that level of functioning. Many have referred to emotions as being on a frequency scale and having energy. So higher frequency emotions are those that are positive and light such as love and joy while lower frequency emotions are those that are dark and heavy such as rage and hatred. If you have a history of unresolved trauma, the chances are that you experience a limited range of emotion.

Clients who have a significant trauma history often struggle with identifying and subsequently regulating their emotions (mostly anger, fear and despair) they are plagued by feelings of unworthiness and subsequently fear that they are not good enough and won't ever be; anger at life for not dealing with the fairly despite their good intentions and all they've been through, and despair because despite their best efforts, they still don't experience the joy and peace that they desire.

The ability to identify your emotions is an important task, but more important is the ability to regulate your emotions. I hate to harp on the impact of early development experiences (not really, I actually love it), but most adults have significant difficulty regulating their emotions and self soothing because they didn't receive adequate modeling of how to do so from a trusted adult. They likely also experienced the effects of loved adult's unregulated emotions in the form of angry outbursts, reactive parenting behaviors and misunderstood consequences for unrelated behaviors. Healthy human behaviors develop in the context of trusted relationships.

This is why it is so difficult for most of us--we've never had healthy trusted relationships within which to learn to regulate our despair, hopelessness, fear, anxiety or even happiness. Yet, In order to get to Peace, we have to make a shift away from dysregulation into healthy regulation. We have to teach ourselves how to know what we're feeling, how to feel our emotions without breaking down and then we have to soothe ourselves so we don't act out in self sabotaging or harmful ways.

As humans, we feel our emotions intensely most times without understanding the reasons why. The part of our brain that deals with emotion is known as the limbic system and is the primitive part of our brain that usually reacts quickly without consulting our problem solving system. Our emotions are also associated with our experience and our memories. Emotions are also closely linked to values: an emotional response could tell you that one of your key values has been challenged.

So often when we have really intense emotions, they are rarely the product of the current situation but an intermingling of our memories, experiences, values and what is happening now. Understanding this link to memory and values gives you the key to managing your emotional response.

Habit to Peace: Practice Letting Your Feelings Come and Go

Take some time to notice your emotional responses and consider what might be behind them, whether values, memories or experiences. Allow your feelings to exist without reacting. Remember that feelings come and go.

Practical Steps to Peace:

1. Be open and accept what is going on around you. Learn to appreciate what is happening and avoid excessive criticism of others or of situations. This is linked to mindfulness, which is about being aware of what is going on in the moment.

2. While you can't change the emotions as they arrive, you can change how you react. The key is to be aware of your emotional response, and understand what might be behind it. That way, you can apply some reason to the situation that you are facing.

3. Give yourself space and time before responding. I find that once you slow your immediate emotional response, you give yourself room to think different thoughts and decrease the intensity of your emotional reaction.

For example, you might ask yourself some questions about possible courses of action, like:

- How do I feel about this situation?
- What do I think I should do about it?
- What effect would that have for me and for other people?
- Does this action fit with my values?
- If not, what else could I do that might fit better?
- Is there anyone else that I could ask about this who might help me?

4 Keys For Making Your Shifts Last

1. Commit to the Long-term. The decision to be different is one of the most powerful choices anyone can make. Most times we get in the way of our own progress because we believe that change is so hard and will take enormous effort. And it will take effort. It will be challenging at the outset but consistency and sustained effort is the key to making your shifts last. Our brain is extremely efficient. At first, our brain doesn't want the change but as we remain steadfast and intentional, our brain adapts to the changes until they become almost automatic.

2. Expect it to be challenging. There is no such thing as the easy way as even when we believe we've found an easy solution, there will always be something missing or something that comes back to bite us. Your best bet is to expect and anticipate that the road will be long. That change is a process and that things will take you time. When you anticipate the process of changing instead of merely the outcome, what happens along the way to change becomes something to look forward to.

3. Make tiny shifts important. As you do the work, I challenge you to be mindful. Be deliberate about remaining focused on

what's changing now—celebrating even the tiniest shifts you experience. When you are able to identify tiny shifts, the journey becomes a beautiful surprise. You are able to savor it. You can release the urgency that you sometimes use as a motivator and that ultimately can lead to discouragement and disappointment when things don't happen fast enough. Remember that it's the accumulation of tiny shifts that make a big change.

4. Take care of you. The shifts that we deal with in this book are shifts that may take years to fully ingrain in your brain, especially since they are beliefs and thought patterns that you have developed and rewarded for years, So please be patient, compassionate and gracious with yourself. Know that when you start, you will experience slip ups and setbacks. That is the nature of the changing brain; you are not difficult and incorrigible—you are human.

About the Author

Susaye Rattigan, PhD is a Clinical Psychologist and Transformational Life Coach for executives and entrepreneurs. She is the owner of Thrive Behavioral Health, a private mental health practice in Montego Bay, Jamaica where she resides with her daughter. She conducts personal development seminars and is a sought after speaker. She can be reached at @drsusaye On all social media platforms.

Also by Susaye Rattigan

Get Back Up: A Guided Journal for Healing From Painful Experiences

Crucial Conversations: The Relationship Deck

The Self Exploration Card Deck: 48 Questions for Reconnecting with Who You Really Are